Along the River 2

More Voices from the Rio Grande

edited by

David Bowles

VAO Publishing
A division of *Valley Artistic Outreach*
4717 N FM 493
Donna, TX 78537
www.vaopublishing.com

ISBN: 978-0615723761

First printed edition: November 2012

Contents

Contributor Biographies

Foreword

VAO Publishing believes that people in our community need venues for their artistic expression. It is essential that human beings have a creative outlet for their dreams, emotions, ideas. A life without art is somehow poorer, so the small regional press works to provide opportunities for self-expression.

The present volume is the second in VAO Publishing's *Along the River* anthology series, a project that showcases the diverse writing talent of south Texas, sampling the language and literature of this region, its peculiar rhythms and accents, the rich culture that it so eloquently encodes.

The contributors to *Along the River 2* range from established authors to emerging talents, from professors to students, from lawyers to housewives and everything in between. Just as varied as the authors are the pieces themselves. In the following pages, thirty-nine voices mingle like the currents of the great river, flowing into deep narrative *resacas* and rushing from lyrical reservoirs. Just as the Río Grande wends its way through basins, *bosques*, deserts, fields—so these poems, stories and essays explore the variegated quiltwork of border culture, streaming somberly through the darkness and coruscating in the light.

In addition to its importance for the burgeoning literary scene in the Río Grande Valley and its environs, this anthology is also an important tool in the promotion of the arts throughout our region. VAO Publishing's parent organization, Valley

Artistic Outreach, was founded in 2010, by a group of artists driven by a shared vision: go into communities throughout the Río Grande Valley and provide art workshops to kids who—because of their socio-economic status or because their schools had abandoned the arts to focus on state testing—had no access to the sorts of horizon-expanding activities that tend to put more affluent students at a distinct advantage.

This mission has resulted in our collaboration with partners throughout the RGB to carry out arts workshops (and to host multiple art exhibits and performances, providing venues for the artistic expression of adults as well). In a time in which federal and state funding for the arts is at a historic low, this anthology series can be a boon to artists and children. With the proceeds from the sale of *Along the River 2*, VAO will continue its dual mission, helping to nourish the seed that the arts can plant in the heart of every member of our community.

By purchasing the book you hold in your hands, you have become a partner in that very worthy endeavor. Thanks!

David Bowles

October 21, 2012

Prose Selections

Snow in the Valley

Peter — *i'm thinking of getting joey _mass effect 2_ for xmas. 2 violent? u cool with it?*
Stella — *ok, he has worse games. i think he'll like it*
Peter — *cool. i'll ship it to your name giftwrapped 4 tree.*
Peter — *also, i'll drive up there 22nd and get joey morning of 23rd 4 laser tag and medieval times, then to ted's xmas eve lunchtime. still works?*

After typing and sending a pressing email, Peter scanned through the Inbox for new "emergencies." He read, "FW: Reminder: Tamalada TODAY." It was forwarded by Marianna—the boss. He opened it, revealing a graphic with festive green and red text wrapped around a 3-D-ish, star-shaped *piñata*. "Noon to 2 p.m., Wednesday, Dec. 16, El Gran Salón."

"Rosa," he said across the aisle, "What is a '*tamalada*'?"

"It's a Mexican Christmas party," she replied, "We eat tamales. UTB has one every year for staff and faculty. It's the president's pet. She always serves everyone."

"Cool. Are you going?"

"Yeah, I think all of us are going."

Noon came. Computers locked, phones forwarded, Peter, Rosa, Marianna, and the rest of the Publications Office crew left Gorgas Hall and its brick, Spanish arches. Warm, moist air blew from the Gulf as they meandered along the *paseo* under ancient live oaks, between Cardenas North and South Halls, toward the

Student Union. Like bees returning to the hive, UT Brownsville personnel squeezed around the lit, giant Christmas tree, went up the mission-like facade's splayed stairs, and entered El Gran Salón. Around the room's edges, noisy workers gathered at white-clothed tables, talking over piled plates. Green and red crepe decorations hung along the walls and from the ceiling. In the room center, two lines straddled a serving station. Peter got in line.

"I am *sooo* ready for break," said Graciela, stepping into line behind him. She looked at him with sideways eyes and a slight smile.

"Yeah, me too," he said, throat a little dry. "Here, let me get that for you," he said, reaching for a plate.

Graciela accepted it, then Peter got one for himself. A server in a black, tux-like outfit spooned some *frijoles* on their plates, then some rice.

"Big plans for Christmas?" she asked.

"Nothing big. I'm driving up to Dallas to see Joey before he goes to his dad's house. Then I'm going to spend Christmas Eve and day at Jim's with his mom and whoever else they're having over."

"You're not going to be with Joey on Christmas?"

"No, he usually goes to his dad's on Christmas Eve day and spends Christmas day at home with Stella and her family."

"That doesn't seem fair. You don't ever get him for Christmas?" she said.

"I'm an EX-stepdad, or whatever. That's the deal," he said evenly and looked away.

The line shuffled again, and Peter and Graciela stood before the university president, serving the tamales. Her black hair back in its customary bun, she smiled at them—regal, motherly, and charming.

"Thank you so much for all your hard work this year," she said as she placed two steaming tamales on each of their plates.

"Thank *you*, ma'am," they said.

Gathering salad, salsa, and sugar cookies—plates precariously balanced between drink- and utensil-holding hands—they stood close a moment in the stuffy crowd.

"I can't decide between two dollhouses for Letty. Will you come by my office and look at them? I need to order one today, or it won't be on time," she said.

"Sure."

Graciela turned, glanced back over her shoulder, and went to sit with the Writing Lab folks. He watched a long minute, then joined his officemates.

After eating tamales—the spice-red, *masa*-crusted husks piled high in the middle of the table—after cookies and hot cocoa, and after the heavy meal had finally slowed conversation, one by one the workers meandered back to their offices or, in some cases, stole home.

Jim — *hey, gotta big question. aunt jane called from michigan. says aunt sarah is poorly, that i'd better come up now if i want to see her...*

Jim — *but ur coming up for xmas. u ok with that? ur gonna be ok on xmas?*

Peter — *sure! take care of your family. love to see you, but that comes first*

Jim — *ok, great. sorry. i'll let you know if something changes*

THE PUBLICATIONS OFFICE CHRISTMAS PARTY WAS THE LAST ORDER of business before the break.

"... on, Donner, on, Blitzen, on, Chewy, on, Tavo, come on Beto!" Peter sang in his best Cheech Marin voice.

"I love that song!" said Rosa, as everyone laughed.

"No, no, no, no!" said someone, "My favorite is 'Pancho Claus,' with the donkeys."

"Pancho Claus! Aieeee!!!" yelled another.

More laughter. More chatter. More cookies.

Marianna plopped down in a chair. "I'm so tired! Javier and I were up late wrapping the kids' presents. I miss the days when they were asleep by 7 p.m.!"

"Oh," said Rosa, "I haven't even really started shopping yet. I have so much to do! The mall is going to be *muy loco* tomorrow."

"I know it!" said Marianna. "Peter, did you get your shopping done?"

"Yeah, a while ago. I didn't have much to buy," he said.

"No?" she asked.

"Nah ... I don't really have much family. Just my stepson, Joey, and some good friends."

"Is Joey coming down?"

"No, I'm going to see him up in Dallas," he said.

The party wound down about 3:30, and folks went back to their desks to finish emails, gather their tupperware and party gifts, shut things down. Peter stayed at his desk, working.

"Aren't you leaving early?" said Marianna. "I won't tell the boss," she joked.

"I'll leave in a bit," he said. "I just have some loose ends I want to tie up before the break. I don't want to leave a mess."

"Well, have a good holiday!" she said, and left.

The front door locked behind her.

Peter — *hey, never heard back. 9 am wednesday still good to pick up joey?*

Stella — *we're flying to vancouver tomorrow morning. will be back jan 2. thought you knew. sorry.*

Peter — *i have to be be back at work that day. what the hell?!*

AN HOUR PASSED. THEN ANOTHER. PETER DOVE FROM WEBSITE TO website. Finally, he left.

His beaten, scratched-up Accord was the last car in the parking lot. Gray, rainy clouds hovered past the tops of the sabal palms. Drizzle. He got in the car and sat a while, looking through the dirty, cracked windshield and tears at the streetlight nimbus swelling in the misty air.

He drove off through the still campus, then on International Boulevard. Mexican holiday shoppers were driving toward the bridge to Matamoros and home. Fake holley festooned the signs of the pawn shops and *casas de cambios*. Night's blackness was ascendant; street and car lights fought weakly against the dark.

Peter drove on to the big H-E-B on Ruben Torres Boulevard. In the crowded store, center displays were piled high with pecans and almonds, bags of dried corn husks, bags of *masa* mix, chocolates. Cakes and pies were stacked double in the bakery. Mothers pushed carts along the crowded aisles, excited children hanging on the baskets, exasperated husbands trailing behind.

He grabbed a few things: a rotisserie chicken, a pecan pie, a can of green beans, a can of cranberry jelly, floss. Long, long checkout lines. He waited.

Then he went "home"—the Value Place extended-stay motel, along the 77 access road. The parking lot was half empty; many guests had already left for the holidays.

Wrestling with groceries and things from work, he went through the long, gray-carpeted hallway past anonymous doors, then entered his monk-like cell. He put food on the counter, floss in the bathroom, shopping bags in the trash.

On the table, he placed a poinsettia as a centerpiece and put his office-party gifts around it—a little stocking with chocolates, a single-serving of gourmet coffee, candy cane, pen, stress ball. He pulled a large, Rubbermaid bin from under the bed and dug around, producing a Yoda ornament wrapped safely in a fuzzy, red Santa hat. It had been a gift the year before from Joey. He unwound the ornament from a the hat, kissed it, and held it a long time before placing it before the poinsettia.

He turned to making dinner. A few minutes later, he removed green beans from the microwave, added steaming spoonfuls to his plate alongside a chicken leg, cranberry jelly, and oatnut bread, which was spread with margarine and garlic salt.

Bean water washed under the other food, soaked the bread's corner.

He sat down with plate and laptop, and ate. The chicken was tender but had a metallic backtaste; yellow fat clung to the bones. The green beans were briny and squelchy; they burned his palate. The bread was soggy. The cranberry jelly tasted slightly of the can. He flipped back and forth between CNN.com, Salon.com, and Facebook. He sucked the gristle off the bones.

Peter tipped the bones into the trash and put the plate into the sink. He rinsed his greasy fingers in scalding water, wiped them on his pants. Then he took to the pie, moving the orange-handled paring knife along its circumference: thin slice? big slice? He settled on a sober quarter, and cut.

He went back to browsing as he ate pie: salted nut; rich, buttery jelly; slight hint of refrigerator and cheap shortening in the crust.

Graciela — *left? i'm going xmas shopping at mall. u want 2 come?*
Peter — *no. kinda busy. thx.*
Graciela — *ok ... :-(*

Closing the laptop lid, he cut himself another slice of pie— this one much bigger than a fourth.

ON CHRISTMAS EVE MORNING, PETER LAY ON HIS RENTED, VALUE Place bed, watching *A Christmas Story*. Again. It was a marathon. On the bedstand stood his big mug of black, sweet coffee and a thick slice of fruitcake. *The Return of the King*, half read, lay face down on the bed amid the rumpled cover. Outside, the sky was overcast. Again. The chill of a freezing drizzle soaked through walls, kept away only by the humming window unit and a fluorescent wall lamp.

Sipping coffee, a little spilled on his shirt, burned his chest. Putting the mug down, he went into the restroom. In the bathroom mirror, he could see patchy silver in the lengthening stubble of his beard and hair.

Big, wet patch on his shirt, he flopped on the bed and took on the coffee again, more successful now, eager for the caffeine to lift his mood. He hadn't left the room in two days. There was nowhere to go.

On TV, the poor kid was wearing the pink bunny suit, his mom haranguing him to keep on his aunt's "gift." Finally, his dad stepped in to defend his boyish honor, talking down the mother. Good thing to have a dad around.

Despite the coffee, he became sleepy and nodded off. Some time passed, not long ... long enough for drool to hit his pillow. His phone chirped.

Graciela — *how is joey? jim? was ur drive 2 dallas ok?*

He sat up, stretched, straightened, looked ahead.

Peter — *didn't make it to dallas. joey in vancouver. jim had family emergency. too far anyway*

Peter stood and went into the bathroom, relieved himself, sat back on the bed. The phone chirped.

Graciela — *oh!? what r u doing for xmas then?*

He sat for a while.

Peter — *not much*
Graciela — *come to my house. we're making tamales.*

Peter put on his street clothes and went outside. Jimmy Stewart's voice from *It's a Wonderful Life* beamed from one of the ground-floor rooms. He walked around the Value Place half a dozen times, the light, cold rain blown at his face by the norther.

He returned to his room, hung his damp sweatshirt over the shower-curtain rod. Then he dialed Graciela, his cheeks hot and cold at the same time.

"I'll come over. How do I get there?"

Peter showered, shaved, and changed. Digging into the bin under his bed, he pulled out the Santa hat that he kept the Yoda wrapped in most of the year. He had bought the hat the first Christmas after he and Stella married, when Joey was little, and worn it every Christmas they were together.

He went to H-E-B, which was packed and frenzied. Twenty-five minutes later, Peter came out with a bottle of Merlot, a green gift bag, and some little presents for Letty—pink plastic Elton John glasses, bubble stuff, and a plastic candy cane full of Hershey's Kisses.

Soon, he pulled up before the house, a stuccoed ranch off Alton Gloor. Gathering the gifts and donning Santa cap, he rang the bell. Christmas hymns played loudly from inside. No answer. He knocked loudly. A few seconds later, Graciela opened the door, her figure cut in designer jeans and a cream-colored top. Hair in soft waves. A smell of perfume. A glass of red wine held cocked.

"You look stunning, m'lady!" he said, bowing slightly and sweeping off the hat.

She looked down slightly a moment, pleased, pursed her red-lipsticked lips, then stepped forward, offering her cheek. Peter kissed it, in the Mexican style—at least as well as his Anglo embarrassment allowed him.

"¡*Feliz Nochebuena!*" she said, "Let me introduce you. But first, put on a smile!" she scolded.

He obliged. She introduced him to her small family.

The tamale-making was under way in earnest. He laid down his burdens and sat at the table.

"See," she said, reaching into the bowl of floating husks, pulling one out, and cupping it in her palm, "You hold it like so. Then take a spoon of *masa*—not too much!—and spread it in one corner. Then you take some fillings—that's pork, that's beans, that's *champiñones* and cheese," she pointed, "and you put a little in. Then you fold up the bottom, roll it, and stand it by the others in the steamer basket."

After his fifth try, Peter didn't make a total mess.

"Graciela has told us so much about you," said her sister.

"I'm surprised you let me in the door," he said.

"Silly! Nothing but good stuff."

A glass of wine was placed in his hand. A platter of *marranitos*, little gingerbread pigs, was pushed toward him. Tamales filled one steamer, then another. Laughter and more laughter as the adults became just a *leetle* drunk.

Graciela allowed Letty to open Peter's gifts, which seemed fair since the Merlot had already been uncorked. In the living room, Letty and her cousin charged at bubbles—until Letty changed the game, running around with a piece of mistletoe, demanding kisses from everyone. It was Peter's turn. After a tiny nod from Graciela, he gave Letty a loud, wet smooch on the cheek, soaking her face. She scowled as she wiped with a napkin, and the adults laughed.

Then, with a vicious twinkle in her eye, she held the mistletoe over Graciela and Peter, and told him, "Now you have to kiss Mamá."

Graciela rolled her eyes and offered a grotesque pucker. He kissed her, quickly. Graciela's sister snickered. Then the others guffawed.

The steamers stuffed and simmering, the adults retired to the living room to watch Mass on TV and patiently await the tamales and a proper dinner.

But the kids had other ideas. The next thing Peter knew, he was dragged into a game of tag through the halls. That is, until he had to play the Evil Queen *and* the Woodsman in Letty's version of *Snow White*. The Evil Queen wore the Elton John glasses, which was fitting. Letty was Snow White, of course. Her cousin played the dwarves, though his Dopey and Sleepy were indistinguishable, and his "dwarven hood" was Peter's Santa hat. Graciela was the Prince, until she begged off. Then the

Prince was played by a stuffed elephant with a voice remarkably like Letty's.

Peter eventually rejoined the adults, who were making un-Catholic speculations about what the priests on TV might—or might not—be wearing under their cassocks.

Suddenly, Letty ran up to Graciela.

"Mamá! Mamá! *Miras*! It's snowing!," she said, pointing to the picture window.

"Yes, Mielita," said Graciela, indulgently patting her daughter's arm, "Santa brought it just for you."

"No! Mamá! No! See!," said an indignant Letty, straining her mother's arm to pull her off the couch and to the window.

Everyone looked. It was, indeed, snowing! On Christmas Eve! In Brownsville! Pure, white powder covered the neighbor's roof and palms, visible across the yard. They walked outside as if just aroused from sleep.

"I don't think it's snowed in the Valley since Abuelo was a boy, maybe a century," said Graciela's sister.

Neighbors streamed out. Letty and her cousin made snow angels. Nearby, the pop-pop-pop of fireworks got an early start.

New flakes caressed Peter's face. Crisp air cleansed his mind, refreshed him.

Letty ran up, holding the Santa hat out.

"Put it on! Put it on!" she said as her cousin laughed.

Peter put on the hat. It was filled with snow, freezing his shaved head. But he stood his ground and stuck out his tongue as Letty and her conspirator ran off giggling.

Graciela stepped beside Peter and placed her cool hand into his, intertwining their fingers. Gripping firmly, he pulled her closer.

Alan Oak

The Body by the Canal

T here's a dead body by the canal."

I glanced up at my brother Fernando. A couple of hours ago I had let him go across the breezeway to Speedy Espericueta's apartment, just to get him out of my hair. It was Friday, but there was no school, so I was stuck babysitting an 11-year-old who seemed to relish getting himself in trouble.

Now here he was, sweaty and out of breath, feeding me a ridiculous line of crap.

"Nando, what the hell, man. I told you not to leave the complex. Mom'll kill me if she knows you went to the canal again."

"You didn't hear me? There's a body there, Oscar. A dead one."

"Yeah, sure there is. Why don't you take a shower or something. You stink."

He shut the door and walked over to the sofa. I dog-eared my book and really looked at him. There was fear in his eyes, genuine horror like I hadn't seen him show since dad left.

"Dude," he said, his voice hoarse, quavering, "I'm not messing with you. We went down to go fishing, me and Speedy. Then we saw them—guy's legs, sticking out of the weeds."

That final detail convinced me. Trying to stay calm, I grabbed the phone and dialed 911. I rattled off a summary of the situation, and the dispatcher said the Pharr PD would send someone by.

Fernando and I went outside. We lived in the projects across the street from the Pharr Community Center, a block of section-8 apartments, the last refuge of the disposed and discarded.

That's what we are, I thought as I looked over the railing at the motley assortment of clunkers in the pitted parking lot. *Discarded*.

"We shouldn't call mom?" Fernando asked.

"No. Last thing she needs is more stress. Don't want her freaking out and leaving work. She'd probably call in sick at the other job, too."

We need to get out of this place, I didn't say. *And for that we need every dime she can scrape together.*

My little brother just shrugged and waited silently by my side. I'd pretty much been his surrogate dad for the past four years, and though he preferred to be all independent, he tended to follow my lead.

A squad car pulled up and we went down the steps to meet the officer, a short, balding man named Acosta. I recognized him from the anti-drug lecture he had given us sophomores a few weeks ago. He didn't seem to remember me, even with my long hair and torn jeans.

Acosta put us in the back, and peering awkwardly through the grilling, Nando guided the cop down to Ridge Road and up the dirt path that led to the canal.

"There it is!" he finally called out. The patrol car bumped to a stop, and Officer Acosta let us out. The heat of the Indian summer made everything hazy, bled color from the vegetation, leaving the meager brush pallid and dead. The hollow whine of cicadas drowned out all other noise—an ominous, predatory rattle. I wiped sweat from my face and followed Nando as he took a few hesitant steps away from the car. For a moment my eyes were overwhelmed by the dusty brightness, but I squinted painfully as my little brother froze up.

And then I saw it.

Thrusting out dumbly onto the hard-packed gravel were two lifeless legs: pale, thin, coated with wiry black hair. One foot was covered by a black nylon sock; the other was bare, and I noticed with a strange sort of nausea that the man had not clipped his toenails in some time.

Acosta quickly turned back to the patrol car, leaning in and grabbing his radio. As if from a great distance, I heard him call for an ambulance and additional officers. The dull hum of the cicadas filled my ears, thrummed in my skull like the low growl of some unseen machinery or massive beast.

I took another step. Nando put his hand on my arm, but I pulled away, closer to the body. I could see more of him, nearly all of his torso. He was wearing black briefs and a white undershirt. Sickly weeds obscured his arms; his face was covered by the low, knotty branches of some thorny bush.

This is death. Abrupt. Meaningless. Dumb. A body, discarded, swallowed by the gaping jaws of nature.

With a superhuman effort, I turned my back on the body, grabbed my brother by the arm and herded him back inside the car. In a few minutes the area was swarming with cops and EMTs. Acosta drove us back to the projects, jotted down Nando's statement. Then he drove away, and that was that.

We learned weeks later that the dead man had been a teacher with AIDS who had nonetheless continued collecting lovers as if such a thing could extend his life. Some of them had learned the truth, and together they had killed him, dumping his body by the canal afterwards.

The sordid details meant nothing to me. They still don't. I close my eyes and I see those legs, that dusty, weed-entangled torso, and I *wish* that I could tell you that the body sits up, a zombie, hungering for my flesh...

...but no, it still lies there in my mind, discarded and forgotten, and in the unbearable silence of that inevitable death the body by the canal devours my very soul.

David Bowles

Lakota Spirits

It was a makeshift deathbed but it would have to do. A proper Lakota bed to die in would be elevated by scaffolding at least four to five feet off the ground. It would be constructed of desiccated tree branches and sticks, dried and ready to burn. The funeral pyre would consume his body and offer his soul to the moon in a raging tower of flames.

That was the covenant of his tribe with the ancient gods. It would be extremely bad luck if George were to dishonor that promise.

But instead of a Lakota bed, George stared at a weather-beaten piece of plywood, supported by six sandstone boulders. It was all the wood he could find, leaning against the side of his son-in-law's garage. He'd gathered kindling wood and stuffed it under the platform, but it still didn't look right.

He removed his straw hat with one hand and used his other to wipe his forehead with a handkerchief. The southwest desert was unforgiving. The temperature yesterday reached 110 degrees and today it felt even hotter. He squinted. Waves of undulating heat danced in the distance where thunderclouds formed then gently blew over the western butte. He retrieved his ceremonial headdress from the bed of the truck and stared at it. He hadn't worn it in ages. The eagle feathers hadn't fallen off but they were sun-bleached and faded. He took off his hat and stuffed it under the plywood. Then, he slipped the headdress onto his head, grabbed his canteen, and chugged a long swig of warm water.

It was dinnertime and he wondered whether anyone at home would notice his absence. If he would've brought his glasses, he would've been able see the hogan about a mile away. Long shadows cast by his pick-up provided some solace. Moving like the ancient man he felt he was, George eased his body down. He sat on the dusty ground and reclined against the front tire. He lowered his head and held his fissured hands before him to study, as if reading the past rather than the future in the lines of his palms. He then closed his eyes and felt the beads of sweat roll down the sides of his face. He never thought his last day on earth would entail such hard work. His labored breathing slowed and he fell into a steady breathing pattern.

He felt his eyelids droop and then close completely. He saw flashes of light on the inside canvas of his eyelids and for a moment, he thought he might be having another one of his diabetic attacks. But he wasn't feeling pain or discomfort as the flashes of red, yellow and white diminished in brightness.

He felt adrift in time and place, his memory sliding from one foggy image to another. When he entered the dreamstate that arises just before sleep, his mind drifted back to his younger days. In his mind's eye he saw himself before he had diabetes, when he was a teenager on the reservation up north. He was healthy back then, no weight issues, no glucose problem and no worries in the world.

Cocooned in his dreams, as a breeze spun filaments of heat around him, George considered the countenance of his dearly departed mother. The mere thought of her gentle features were enough to comfort him. She had been proud of him when he began to run on the high school track team and win some races. She said his ancient ancestors ran a lot. She said long ago, they did not have horses and people had to run.

Down here in Texas, George was the half-breed in his tribal community, the kid who belonged neither to one tribe or another. His mother was Navaho and his father was Lakota Sioux. He never got a straight answer from either parent as to how they met. According to his mother, their romance blossomed at a pow-wow when George's father bought her a beer, but his father disagreed. His memory said he saved her from a burning village.

George's vision then shifted to his twelve year-old grandson, Walks-on-Clouds. His Anglo name was Billy James, but George preferred to call him by his traditional Native American name. His Anglo name was too bland for George's liking.

At one time George had big plans for himself and his grandson. He felt a need to take him to the Grand Canyon and expose him to the majesty of The Great Father's creation. And he wished Billy would become a runner like he'd been, maybe even become a state champion. But Walks-on-Clouds was still too young to start running races. His little legs tired just chasing after chickens in the back yard.

Somehow, even through his closed eyelids, George saw in the distance a couple of dust devils dance around each other in the undulating heat waves. They'd close the distance between them and then suddenly separate, as if the spirit of one was afraid to touch the essence of the other. Then, they'd repeat the cycle, daring each other to spin closer. This was his universe, hot, dusty and beautiful and George knew he was going to miss it.

The whirling wind and the free-spirited dance of the dust reminded George of the day his father took him to his first ghost dance ceremony. It happened on a sweltering, August night at the reservation. George was about the same age as Walks-on-Clouds.

"How come they have to build a fire?" George asked his father. "It's still hot from this afternoon."

His father was a sturdy man and he answered in his naturally deep voice. "It is said that the spirits come when there is light from the fire to reveal the way through the darkness of their world."

"What spirits, Father?"

"Many spirits, not just one or two. It's the spirits of our slain warriors, our family relatives that have passed to the other side and it's the spirit of our gods. They come to remind us of our legends and our determination to be free."

"Free from what?"

His father gazed down at George then went down on one knee. He looked George directly in the eyes. "You're still young, son, but you're old enough to hear this. Our people are not happy living on reservations, like we do. We never have been, since we were rounded up like animals and penned in many years ago. You will learn in school about the many treaties made and broken by the white man, causing us great pain and anguish. The ghost dance fortifies our resolve to wait out the white man till the day when we re-take our lands. We dance to stay in touch with those spirits. Watch, you'll see."

George didn't know what all that meant, but it sounded serious to him so he decided to only observe from that point on. And he was glad he did.

The Lakota dancers were decked out in their traditional regalia, not the fake feathers and American flag colors of today's Native Americans. Real eagle feathers and leather headdresses adorned the men. Some wore little noise-making trinkets around their ankles. There were no women. The face paint gave the dancers a fierce warrior look.

When the pounding of the drums began, George was startled. Soon, however, he sensed a strange, intoxicating power in the mere observation of the dance. The chants led by Black Elk mesmerized him. The firelight, the hypnotic beating of the drums and the shadows of the dancers all moved in rhythm against the backdrop of the surrounding trees. Through some magical means, he did feel as though he'd connected to otherworldly beings. By the end of the night, he knew he'd remember the ghost dance and his father's words forever, and he did.

It might have been a few hours and it might have been more. George wasn't sure, but a cool breeze eventually brought him to his awakened senses. He was still on the ground but while he slept, he'd somehow rolled onto his side. He pushed himself up to a sitting position and considered his makeshift Lakota bed. If anyone else from his tribe saw his preparations to die, they might just laugh at his amateurish structure. He didn't care. Life was over for him now.

His only son had gone into the Navy years ago. When he came back to visit, he'd brought his "significant other" to meet George. When George figured out what was going on between his son and his male friend, he was heartbroken. He felt he'd been disgraced.

If his wife was still alive, there might be something to live for, but she too, was gone – breast cancer. In his naïveté, he didn't think Native American women died from such a malady. Now, of course, he knew a different, painful truth.

To make things worse, Doc told George, "Your liver's not working right. You ought to quit drinking alcohol." Yeah, like that was going to happen.

If there was anything to live for now, it was his daughter's son, Walks-on-Clouds. His mere presence brought joy to George's heart. Maybe, just maybe, Walks-on Clouds would live to see the day when the Lakota would regain their lost tribal lands.

George grabbed onto the truck's fender and eased himself up. It was time to travel to the other side. If it was possible, he'd come back and visit his family through the ghost dance.

From the backpack in the cabin of the truck, George retrieved a butane lighter. He was too old to start a fire with sticks or a flint. Besides, the spirits probably didn't really care how the flames came to be. The important thing was the human sacrifice.

George took his place on the plywood and stared at the darkening skies. He'd picked this particular night to turn to ashes because of the full moon in the sky. Ironically, just last night he'd been telling Walks-on Clouds, about the mythical man on the moon. A hoot owl made a screeching sound not far away.

His body shivered from his low back up to his neck. How long had he been out here?

George lit the lighter and while remaining in a prone position, he reached to the side of the wood to light the kindling. The flame flickered and when he stretched a little farther, it went out. He sat up and studied his predicament. All the good kindling and the driest part of the wood was at the foot of his bed. Should be rearrange everything and bring the kindling closer? Maybe he could make a torch on a long stick and reach the kindling that way.

Since he was already tired and anxious to leave this world, George chose the easiest option. He would light the fire with the wood and kindling right where it was, but without him on the bed. He'd make sure the fire was raging and then he'd jump onto the platform. It might hurt, but he wouldn't be around much longer to feel the pain anyway.

Sure enough, the kindling worked fine, though the plywood took longer to be consumed by the flames. Seconds before he was ready to jump onto the bed, the intense heat caused George to experience extreme dizziness. He reeled backward and leaned against the door of the truck. His heart was pounding. *I can't die this way*, he thought, *I'm supposed to be in the fire.*

With his back pressed against the truck, George slid down to the ground. It was indeed over. He was convinced his dreams hadn't been dreams at all. They'd been final visions of all that was dear to him, even his queer son. The pounding in his heart was now working its way to his head. The veins in his temples throbbed. He closed his eyes and bid the world farewell, rendering his soul to the ancients.

George expected everything to vanish, the feel of the fire's heat, the coolness of the night air, the pain in his heart and head and, of course, his consciousness. But something else happened. He heard what he assumed was an angel's voice.

"Papa? Papa George?"

George pushed opened his eyes and, for a moment, he thought maybe he had died and gone to the next world. Standing before him was Walks-on-Clouds.

"Papa George?"

"Walks-on-Clouds, what are you doing here?"

"Mama told me to find you. I ran here." He pointed to the tire tracks behind the truck. "I followed your tracks. You forgot your insulin. I brought it for you," said the little angel, reaching toward George with a hypodermic needle in his outstretched hand.

"Oh, thank you, thank you." said George as he hugged the boy. He was struck by the powder fresh smell and feel of Walks-on-Clouds. There was something unique and impossibly sweet in the smell of a little boy. It evoked images of innocence and laughter and the joy of endless possibility.

George took the insulin and reclined against the truck. He deliberated whether to inject the solution into his veins or just lapse into a diabetic coma and die. But there was no way he could wreak such pain and sorrow upon his precious grandson.

Walks-on-Clouds focused on the raging blaze. "What's the fire for? Are you cooking something?"

George grinned and thought about his now-obsolete plans to pass over to the spirit world. "No, I was just building a little bonfire."

Walks-on-Clouds sat down next to George and looked into the flames. "Papa?"

"Yes?"

"I like the feathers in your hat."

George took a deep breath. "It's a warrior's headdress, a holy relic, a cultural artifact." He noticed the frown on his grandson's face. "You know what?"

"What?"

A cool breeze moved through the sage around them, whispering just loud enough to obscure the crackling of the blaze. "My father used to tell me Indian stories of magic around a fire like this. Wanna hear the one about the Lakota spirits?"

Michael Pacheco

Tierra

Un niño se perdió en un bosque. Un bosque triste, tétrico y tenebroso lleno de árboles flacos y desnutridos con brazos como de esqueleto y cabellera color púrpura. Un hermoso cuervo con plumas de diamantes negros lo seguía mientras de su pico inclemente brotaban *Las letanías de Satán* en francés antiguo. El niño aterrado comenzó a correr, sus pies desnudos se enredaban entre la dura maleza que los raspaba y los hacía sangrar. El niño corría y corría invadido por el terror de este paisaje *Burtoniano*. El ave siniestra que seguía volando justo encima de su cabeza gritaba, y el "¡Oh Satán!" retumbaba entre las venas gruesas de los troncos vetustos que crujían con el viento como la leña cruje al ser vencida por el fuego. En su escape, un río de sustancias amarillentas se atravesó en su camino. La corriente arrastraba cientos de peces muertos, todos flotando sobre la aterradora superficie de navajas y olvido. Sin pensarlo, el niño dio un salto infructuoso intentando cruzar el holocausto bajo sus pies. Cayó en las aguas purulentas y se vio rodeado de muerte, despojos humanos y cabezas cercenadas. Asustado y casi ahogándose, salió del río a gatas, tosiendo y dando gritos estridentes como animal de rastro implorando misericordia. Se tumbó en la hierba opaca y se dio cuenta que el ave infernal había desaparecido. Se incorporó. Volvió la mirada y el bosque era un monstruo gigantesco hecho de fuego y explosiones, de balas y granadas: el infierno creado por el hombre. Una gran bandera de tonos camuflados desplegaba la leyenda, "Bienvenidos a T".

Alejandro Fernández Cabada

Land

A child was lost in a forest. A sad, gloomy and dark forest full of scrawny, malnourished trees with skeletal limbs and purple hair. A beautiful raven with feathers like black diamonds followed him, its stern beak spouting *The Litanies of Satan* in Old French.The terrified boy darted away, his bare feet becoming tangled in the rough underbrush that scraped and made them bleed.The boy ran and ran, overwhelmed by the terror of the *Burtonian* landscape. The sinister bird wheeled through the air just above his head screaming, and its "Oh Satan!" echoed among the thick veins of hoary trunks that creaked in the wind as wood does upon being consumed by fire. As he tried to make his escape, he discovered a river of yellowish ooze crossing his path. The current dragged hundreds of dead fish along, all floating on a terrifying surface of blades and oblivion.Without thinking, the child made an unsuccessful leap, attempting to cross the Holocaust roiling below. He fell into the festering water and was surrounded by death, human remains and severed heads. Scared and nearly drowning, the boy crawled out of the river, coughing and screaming like a hunted animal crying for mercy. He lay on the dark grass and realized the infernal bird was gone. He sat up.He looked about him and found the forest had become a giant monster made of fire and explosions, bullets and grenades: a man-made hell. A large banner dappled in camouflage tones bore the legend, "Welcome to T."

(English translation by David Bowles)

Doña Lipa

Doña Lipa era una mujer como de ochenta años. Era delgada y baja de estatura, de piel pintada por el sol y manos largas cubiertas de paño. Sobre su espalda el peso de una joroba inclinaba, ligeramente, su cuerpo hacia el lado izquierdo. Usaba vestidos negros y una pañoleta percudida para cubrir sus largos cabellos blancos dando siempre un aspecto de enlutada. Sus ojos eran como túneles profundos y miles de arrugas dibujaban en su rostro un pasado tormentoso. Vivía en una casa vieja, descolorida y carcomida por el tiempo, de paredes agrietadas y grandes ventanales taciturnos como los ojos de un búho. Era una casa que daba una apariencia de tristeza, soledad y abandono lo cual representaba de manera perfecta la vida de su dueña.

Recuerdo que había rumores en la colonia de que Doña Lipa había sido alguna vez una mujer muy perversa. Algunos decían que practicaba la magia negra y otros decían que era una hechicera muy poderosa. Ciertas personas se atrevían a decir que desde niña había sido consagrada al príncipe de la potestad del aire y por eso tenía tanta vida y poder. Según las damas de la iglesia, Doña Lipa tenía más de doscientos años, pero ni siquiera los curas que habían pasado por la parroquia a lo largo de varias décadas, habían indagado en la vida de la misteriosa mujer. Todo esto a mí me parecía una gran historia, un "cuento de rancho" que sólo la gente con muy poco intelecto podía creer y en lugar de asustarme me causaba una curiosidad profunda. Mis

Doña Lipa

D oña Lipa was a woman of about eighty. She was thin and small in stature, her skin browned by the sun and her long hands covered with ratty lace. On her back the weight of a hump bent her body slightly to the left. She wore black dresses and covered her long white hair with a yellowed scarf as if in constant mourning. Her eyes were deep tunnels and thousands of wrinkles carved a stormy past into her face. She lived in an old house, bleached and decayed by time, with cracked walls and large windows taciturn as the eyes of an owl. The house had a look of sadness, loneliness and abandon, a perfect representation of its owner{s existence.

I remember there were rumors in the neighborhood that Doña Lipa had once been a very wicked woman. Some said she practiced black magic while others added she was a very powerful sorceress. A few dared to say that as a child she had been consecrated to the Prince of the Powers of the Air and for that reason had so much life and power. According to the ladies of the church, Doña Lipa was over two hundred years old, but not even the many priests who had been through the parish over several decades had delved into the life of the mysterious woman. This all seemed to me a great story, a *"cuento de rancho"* that only people with limited intellect could believe; instead of scaring me, the legend awakened deep curiosity in me. I burned inside to really know who this lady was or had been.

adentros ardían por saber realmente quién era o quién había sido esta señora.

Por las tardes la extraña anciana vendía dulces en su casa. Las madres aterradas le tenían prohibido a sus hijos meterse a esa morada para comprar golosinas. A mí me parecía de cierta forma admirable y me producía ternura que una viejecita aislada del mundo moderno quisiera ganarse unos cuantos pesos y alegrar sus días sombríos viendo y escuchando las sonrisas de niños que, inocentemente, la visitaban todas las tardes para colmar de azúcar la leche en sus delicados dientes, sin juzgarla o verla como una mujer maléfica. Las madres nerviosas y preocupadas obligaban a sus hijos a que fueran mejor al Oxxo, a la farmacia México o por lo menos con Balde, a la tiendita de la esquina. Lo que las madres no sabían era que en esas tiendas no vendían las golosinas que Doña Lipa ofrecía a sus pueriles clientes. Con ella podían comprar colaciones, huevitos confitados, conitos de cajeta y chicles Totito, entre otras golosinas diferentes que los niños no conocían y les parecían deliciosas. Se decía que conservaba todos los dulces en frascos de vidrio y que los vendía de forma individual sacando cada dulce con sus manos y recibiendo las monedas de los niños al mismo tiempo combinando dulces y bacterias en la superficie oscura de sus palmas. Algunos decían que no eran dulces, que lo que guardaba en los frascos eran ojos y dientes humanos y que por algún conjuro maligno hacia que los niños ingirieran las partes humanas. Una tarde fría de diciembre decidí ir a investigar por mi propia cuenta qué era lo que pasaba en esa casa y a ver a la famosa mujer que al paso de los años era considerada, por centenares de personas, una bruja malévola y perversa.

Al estar frente a su casa, una extraña sensación se apoderó de mí. No sé explicarlo con exactitud, pero era como si los dos ventanales me observaran de una forma violenta y me ordenaran que me alejara. Por un momento me detuve y observé a mi alrededor. La distancia entre la calle y la puerta sucia y descarapelada de la casa era de unos ocho metros. Ocho metros que parecían ocho kilómetros. Había árboles gigantescos de troncos

In the evening the strange old woman sold sweets at home. Terrified mothers had forbidden their sons to go inside that home to buy candy. It seemed to me in some ways admirable and sweet that an old woman so isolated from the modern world would want to earn a few pesos and brighten kids' dark days, delighting in the smiles of children who innocently visited her every evening to sugarcoat their delicate teeth, without judging or seeing her as an evil woman. Nervous, worried mothers forced their children to pick up snacks at Oxxo, Mexico Pharmacy, or even with Balde, at his shop on the corner. What mothers did not know was that these stores do not sell the treats that Doña Lipa offered her prepubescent clientele. From her they could buy snacks, candy eggs, caramel cones and Totito bubblegum, among other diverse goodies that the children were unfamiliar with but that looked delicious. The rumor was that she kept her sweets in glass jars and sold them by the piece, drawing each candy out with her hands and accepting the children's coins at the same time, combining sweets and bacteria on the dark surface of her palms. Some said they were not candies, that what was in the bottles were human eyes and teeth that through some evil spell she made the children eat these macabre bits. A cold December afternoon I decided to investigate on my own what exactly was happening in that house and to see the famous woman who over the years had been considered, by hundreds of people, an evil and wicked witch.

Standing in front of her house, a strange feeling came over me. I cannot explain it precisely, but it was as if the two front windows glared at me violently, ordering me to stay away. For a moment I paused and looked around me. The distance between the street and the filthy, peeling door was about 25 feet. Those twenty-five feet seemed five miles. There were gigantic trees with ancient trunks, which told me that the land had been inhabited for many decades by Doña Lipa, her parents and maybe by her grandparents and who knows who else. The house was very old, one those houses that exude the darkest secrets of families. Houses whose eyes tire of witnessing so many stories and

arcaicos, lo cual me indicaba que ese terreno llevaba muchas décadas habitado por Doña Lipa, sus padres y posiblemente sus abuelos y quién sabe quién más. Era una casa antiquísima, de esas casas que respiran los secretos más oscuros de las familias. Esas casas que tienen la vista cansada de ver tantas historias e histerias. Esas casas que conservan esquirlas de sangre seca entre las grietas del frío mosaico. Casas que quizá tienen la muerte penetrada entres sus paredes.

Caminé vacilante hasta que llegué a la puerta. Toqué tres veces. Nadie abrió. Esperé unos segundos y volví a tocar tres veces. Nada. De pronto escuché a la distancia una risa extraña, se oía despacio, pero pude percibir que era una risa de mujer. Perplejo, traté de ignorar el incidente, pero era demasiado tarde, el pánico empezó a explorar mi piel. ¿Acaso todos los rumores que había escuchado desde niño eran verdad? ¿Era Doña Lipa en realidad una bruja maldita que devoraba niños y se daba festines con los ojos y frágiles cráneos de las inocentes criaturas?

A mis espaldas había un gran árbol de aspecto tenebroso y lúgubre similar a los árboles que se pueden encontrar en ilustraciones del terror gótico de la Inglaterra del siglo diecinueve. Escuché claramente el aleteo de un ave y el crujir de las ramas por el inesperado movimiento. Sutilmente giré mi cabeza y dirigí la mirada hacia las ramas del árbol. Lo que vi me produjo un escalofrío penetrante. Sentí que perdía la fuerza en mis rodillas y el pulso se me aceleró de manera incontrolable. Ahí estaba, sobre una rama que amenazaba con quebrarse, un espantoso pájaro gris. Era de proporciones gigantescas como un cóndor de los Andes con la fuerza para levantar con sus garras a algún niño desafortunado. Su plumaje era cenizo, opaco con la apariencia de un trapeador asqueroso y maloliente. Los grandes ojos vidriosos tenían un brillo agudo y eran de un tono amarillento y rojizo con las venas reventadas que le daba un aspecto macabro de maldad demoniaca. Su pico era largo y puntiagudo y cuando lo abría se podían ver hileras de pequeños dientes como un serrucho. Con su mirada diabólica me observaba cautelosamente como advirtiéndome que no me moviera.

hysteria. Houses that conserve flakes of dried blood in the cracks of the cold tile. Houses in which death may have penetrated the very walls.

I walked hesitantly until I reached the door. I knocked three times. Nobody answered. I waited a few seconds and once again knocked three times. Nothing, Without warning I heard a distant, strange laughing. It was muted, but I could make out a woman's tones. Puzzled, I tried to ignore the incident, but it was too late: panic began to crawl along my skin. What if all the rumors I'd heard since childhood were true?Was Doña Lipa actually a damnable witch who ate children, feasting on the eyes and fragile skulls of innocents?

Behind me was a large tree of dark and gloomy aspect, much like those trees one finds in Gothic horror illustrations from nineteenth-century England. Clearly I heard the fluttering of wings and the creak of branches as they unexpectedly moved. Carefully I turned my head and looked up into the branches of the tree. What I saw sent a shiver skittering along my spine. My knees weakened; my pulse accelerated uncontrollably. There it sat, on a branch that groaned beneath the weight as if ready to snap: a hideous grey bird. The creature was of gigantic proportions, like an Andean condor, with the strength to easily snatch up an unfortunate child with its talons. Its plumage was ashen, dull-looking like a filthy, stinking mop . Those large glassy eyes gleamed sharply, yellowish red, with burst blood vessels that lent the bird a macabre aspect of demonic evil. Its beak was long and pointed; when it opened, you could see rows of small teeth like a saw. With devilish gaze it watched me closely, as if warning me not to move.

Suddenly it let loose a laugh that must have been heard in the deepest regions of hell. It laughed and laughed like a deranged old woman. To this very day I cannot forget that sinister cackle. Terror overwhelmed me. I wanted to run, but my legs wouldn't move. Waves of cold rushed down my back, all sound muted by my intense fear. I was deaf, could not hear anything. But I could see that damned bird, beating its wings vio-

De pronto soltó una carcajada que debe haber retumbado hasta el mismo infierno. Reía y reía como una anciana trastornada. Era una risa siniestra que hasta el día de hoy no he podido olvidar. El terror me tenía invadido, quería correr, pero mis pies no respondían. Una cascada de hielo escurría por mi espalda y mi sentido del oído se vio interrumpido por una sordera aplastante. Me quedé sordo, no escuchaba nada. Sólo veía al maldito pájaro que agitaba sus alas de forma violenta al mismo tiempo que me descarnaba con su mirada. De pronto empezó a llover y el pájaro levantó el vuelo. Un trueno ensordecedor me sacó del trance y mi oído regresó. Escuché el cerrojo de la puerta y la perilla giró.

La puerta se abrió lentamente...

Alejandro Fernández Cabada

lently as it flayed me to the very soul with its grim gaze. Rain began to fall of a sudden, and the bird wheeled away in flight. Deafening thunder shook me from my trance and my hearing returned. I heard the rattle of the door latch. The doorknob turned.

The door opened slowly...

(English translation by David Bowles)

Una mañana...

Todavía caliente, la cacha de la pistola pesaba toneladas en la mano despavorida de la mujer que yacía inerte de rodillas en la alfombra. Confundida, un timbre ensordecedor carcomía sus oídos bloqueando todo el ruido a su alrededor. El olor a pólvora se filtraba por las cavidades aterradas de su nariz. Su rostro empapado de sudor, lágrimas y miedo, pánico incontrolable. Por la esquina de su ojo derecho veía una sombra que se movía sin control para todos lados de forma animada y violenta. Alzó su mirada y sobre una mesa de centro vio dos tazas que humeaban, probablemente, té de zacate de limón. Una taza era negra, la otra era blanca y estaba manchada de *lipstick* rojo, un rojo vibrante, vulgar. La mujer observaba y trataba de recobrar la calma. Giró la cabeza hacia la derecha y la sombra incontenible tomó forma. Levantó la pistola una vez más y de un certero disparo en el pecho, mató al Doberman que luchaba por romper la cadena que lo aprisionaba. En cuestión de segundos ya no ladraba sino se retorcía como serpiente sobre la superficie de fibras verdes.

La mujer se levantó y caminó hacia la cocina, abrió el refrigerador y sólo había una mohosa jarra con agua y un enorme pedazo de piña echada a perder. La tomó entre sus manos y comenzó a devorarla rápidamente, con mucha ansiedad, como si tuviera un apetito voraz. El sabor era asqueroso, pero por alguna extraña razón, seguía hundiendo los dientes sobre la textura amarillenta de la fruta y al pasar la pulpa sentía como su pa-

One Morning...

Still hot, the butt of the gun weighed tons in the petrified hand of the woman still frozen on her knees on the carpet. She blinked in confusion, a deafening ring gnawing at her ears, blocking all sound around her. The smell of gunpowder insinuated itself into her fear-widened nostrils. Her face was bathed in sweat, tears and fear, twisted by uncontrollable panic. From the corner of her right eye she saw a shadow jerking violently in all directions, completely out of control. She lifted her gaze and saw, sitting on a coffee table, two cups steaming the air, probably lemongrass tea. One cup was black, the other white, stained with red lipstick, a vibrant and vulgar sort of red. The woman observed the room, trying to calm down. She turned her head to the right and the uncontainable shadow coalesced. She raised the pistol once more and, with a well-aimed shot to the chest, killed the Doberman that was struggling to break the chain that restrained it. In a matter of seconds the dog had stopped its barking and was twisting like a snake upon the green fibers.

The woman got up and walked to the kitchen. She opened the refrigerator: there was only a moldy jug with water and a huge piece of spoiled pineapple. She took it in her hands and began to devour it quickly, anxiously, as if driven by a voracious appetite. The taste was disgusting, but for some strange reason she kept sinking her teeth into the yellow texture of the fruit

ladar se escaldaba, pero también sentía que sus adentros se pudrían y ella se convertía en una con el pedazo de fruta repugnante. De pronto, un estallido. Súbitamente el pedazo mordisqueado de piña cayó sobre el mosaico. Mares de oro rojo inundaron el piso y continuaron devorando la piña que flotaba a la deriva en un charco de sangre.

Alejandro Fernández Cabada

pulp; as she swallowed the pulp, it was as if her palate were scalded, her guts rotten, her entire beings converted into a piece of nasty fruit. Suddenly, a roaring burst of sound. Unexpectedly, the gnawed bit of pineapple fell to the tiled floor. A sea of red gold flooded the floor and continued devouring the pineapple that floated adrift upon a pool of blood.

(English translation by David Bowles)

Birth Story

Three to five minutes, regularly spaced, that's when the book said she should go. She knew the line by heart, but still it felt reassuring to see it there, in black and white. She should call her mother, she knew she should. That was the plan, but as soon as the first real one came, she had known that she would not call. She had known that she had always known that she would not.

The next one waited until she was in the car. She gripped the steering wheel and pushed her back into the driver's seat. When it had passed, she started the car. She was not the praying sort, but she said one anyway.

Lord, let there be nobody on the road.

It was summer, and though it had rained most of the day, the night was clear. The full moon was at its zenith. She thought of the *abuelas* at work, the ones that knew these sorts of things or claimed to, saying that babies liked to be born three days before or after *la luna llena*. She wasn't superstitious either, but she had laughed when she looked at her calendar and saw the clean white circle imprinted on her due date.

The book said it was good to have a visualization. It suggested a flower opening, but she realized now she had no idea what that looked like, not really. She tried to visualize her body as the moon waxing, its light opening up to the earth.

When the next one came, she took her foot off the accelerator, trying to keep her eyes focused on the moonlit point where the road met the horizon. She tried to think about the pain, so different from all the other kinds of pain she had ever experienced. She hoped the wall of her thinking could hold back some measure of its force.

Exquisite. That was the word her mind had circled around, buzzard-like, until at last it had materialized on her tongue. Exquisite, like the inner workings of a watch, or the pattern of ice on a window pane. Its edges were so sharp and defined, no crescendo or decrescendo, just fortissimo, an electric shock sizzling through her entire body, then subito piano, as if nothing had ever happened.

She decided to drive as fast as she could in between. When the needle quivered past ninety, the little car shook violently. Never in all her life had she driven so fast, but she pressed down more on the accelerator. She had no idea how fast she was going when the next one came, only that she had almost stopped by the time that it was over. Her stomach seized up. She would not throw up in the car, she told herself. Anything, anything, but that.

There was no shoulder, but she pulled as far over as she could and left her flashers on. She got out of the car and felt her way down to the marshy grass at the bottom of the ditch. She had hoped to be back in the car before the next one. When it came, down there in the grass, there was nothing to lean against.

No time to think. She spread her legs shoulder-length apart and pushed her feet down into the mud. The pain subsided for an instant, as if having her feet rooted was grounding the electric circuit of her body. Then she felt a primal cry leaving her throat, so unlike her voice that she wondered momentarily if it had emitted from her at all. She was not a flower opening. She was not the moon waxing. Her entire body was being ripped apart by invisible talons, from the inside out.

She kept her eyes focused on the horizon and wondered if she would ever be whole again.

Daniel Tyx

Evil Children among Us

We are born without a care in the world, we are born with innocence, and it is our environment that creates us. We do not know right from wrong at birth; no, we learn it. Sometimes just the mere word of our kryptonite can render us weak.

While reading David Rice's short story collection *Heart Shaped Cookies and Other Stories* (Bilingual Review Press, 2011), one story struck a chord with me: "El Cucuy." Nostalgia and forgotten childhood scares kicked in. Hairs were standing, blood was rushing, pupils were dilated, and my heart was racing. Rice's story takes place in Edcouch, where he grew up. In "El Cucuy," two boys are described as horrible children by their family maids, and even one says they may have the devil inside them. The misbehaving children think they are unstoppable and like seeing their maids quit. No matter what tactic the maids try—mean stares, yelling, threats, bribes, begging, and the occasional crying—nothing works on these devil-spawn kids, not until their last maid, Cata. She uses their naïve ways as an advantage; she goes deep inside their psyche and taps into their inner, darkest fear of el cucuy. Cata portrays el cucuy as a vicious creature with long claws, pointy ears, and red or yellow eyes, who can sense when a child misbehaves. And when the child misbehaves, the cucuy will get them!

Although Cata's tactics work on the boys, her method is not the greatest way to make a child listen. Fear is not necessary and can cause lasting trauma for the child. What if the child's cucuy is a clown, and later, he has a phobia of them, without knowing why it happened? Think of the parties the child will miss, the circus invites from their friends they will excuse themselves from. Not to mention the lack of trust the kid might have. So no, I don't agree with scaring children in order to have them behave well.

"El Cucuy" in Rice's story should be recognized as an archetype. Archetypes are universal symbols across many cultures that everyone can relate to. Many people can connect to fear of a creature of the night like the boogeyman, zombie, the pixie, la *lechuza*, etc. Xavier Garza, from Rio Grande City, also depicts *el cucuy* in books such as *Creepy Creatures and Other Cucuys*. It is a creature, yes, and it varies drastically from household to household; but it always has the same meaning of a creature that scares little kids from misbehaving, and it sure worked on me when I was a little girl.

When I was about four or five, I was a brat. I would cry, I would yell, I would throw things around for anything. I remember one time I colored my cousin's walls because she took my 64-color Crayola box. Boy, was I mad. My mom said I was just young, and my dad did not believe in spanking, but my grandfather did not care. He wanted to scare the brat out of me.

I was raised in Mexico in a ranch in the middle of nowhere. It was just my grandparent's house and land going on for miles on end. Beautiful, bright, yellow sunflower fields in the day looked like standing corpses at night. Strong standing and vibrant green trees were like a witch's hand. My pet pig, Bertha (cliché, I know), cute and pink in the day; however, don't ever tell me to look at her at night because she looked like a gremlin. I love the ranch that raised me, really I do, but it fostered probably the worst scares of my life.

Like I said, I was a rotten kid when I was young; maybe this is why I disagree with scaring kids to behave. The ranch, although isolated by land, was active. People came over all the time, mostly to see my grandfather, and when I was around I tried my best not to get in the way of his business. But me being a fun loving kid, I was chasing the ducks which was a big no-no since they tend to leave the ranch and never come back; not only that but they went to my grandfather's area. I was told not to. I was scared. I love my grandfather, but I was scared of him. He was a tall man with boots, a cane, and a cowboy hat. You knew he had a lot of power, and although he loved me unconditionally, he knew that I had to be straightened out. He got very close to me, and I got very scared.

"*M'ija*, do you want me to tell you a story?" My grandfather asked.

"YES!" Scared as I was, he had the best stories, and I was not going to pass that up.

"You know these are old lands, right? Well, a long time ago, before your tío Tanito was even born, there would be a circus over there by the big tree. You see it isn't like those small circus now. No, they had big animals. They had hippos, giraffes, lions, and a bear! They were all three times the sizes of today's animals. The ring master had a baboon, and he was a feisty little thing. He would go up to people and play with their hair, shake hands with kids, and would take his master's hat away. Then one day, the chango went mad! He bit off the hand of his master, and some of the audience, but they could not catch him." My grandfather paused to take a sip of his coffee, and he could tell that I was scared.

"He escaped and is hiding in these lands of ours. You can sometimes see him at the big tree, or the elementary school scaring little kids into behaving well for their teacher. They say you can hear him at night where we keep the lambs, and I hear from my workers all the time that they saw the chango. He isn't like any other baboon, no. He is taller, stronger, and faster. His eyes, you can tell the Devil is inside of him, and his hair is as dark as night so you won't know that he is there in the same room as you. He goes around the pueblo to hear of little kids misbehaving and will haunt them. Remember when you lost your Barbie doll?"

I was petrified by this point, my eyes bulged and watery. I just wanted to run to my mom. But with the strength I had, I nodded yes. I remembered losing my Barbie doll.

"He took her, along with other toys, to let the children know that he is there. Some little boys and girls listen, but others like a certain little five-year-old I know, don't. The chango waits until you are alone." He paused, and I was about to cry. "AND EATS YOU." My grandfather jolted to my direction and grasped his hands around my small arms; firm enough to grab, but gentle enough to know he was messing around. I was bawling by this point, and started yelling that I would be good. At this point, my mother got me and tried to calm me down. She asked my grandfather what happened. His reply: "You'll thank me."

I did not do a single bad thing since then. I no longer wrote on walls, chased the ducks, or talked back to my elders. I even started helping around the house and the ranch, and became the model daughter and granddaughter. As I got older, I got wiser. Although I knew it was a legend around the town, I did my research and there was a monkey that actually bit his master and escaped around the time my grandpa said. The only thing though, they found it lying with two little stab wounds on its neck and its blood sucked dry two weeks later....

Brianda Salinas

Creating a Self-Conscious Literary World in South Texas

Works by David Rice, Gloria Anzaldúa, Rolando Hinojosa, and "The Trinity"

My wife, Erika Garza, is a poet from Elsa, Texas, a small, depressed farming community that used to be home to the Rotel tomato cannery and other light industry. She grew up smelling onions, cilantro, tomatoes, and jalapenos from the Rotel cannery. The railroad ran behind her house, and when she was a child, it was busy hauling out packed vegetables and manufactured goods. She writes about this south Texas border town in many of her poems which are, as far as I know, the only poetry written about that bygone era and place.

Today the railroad tracks are gone, sold as scrap metal, and the town has no industry thanks to fat tax breaks that encouraged businesses to relocate overseas or in Mexico. Others say it was the doing of Chente Polvos, local brujo, who cursed the Rotel cannery when he was fired from his job there. Now, a man in a trench coat haunts the remains of the railroad beds where children collect bits of flint and wonder where they come from and weeds grow in the cracks of the monolithic loading docks that load and unload nothing. Most people in Elsa today work for the always-under-investigation school system (it is also one of the poorest school districts in the country) or are in the adult daycare or funeral business.

Recently, though, Elsa native and actor Valente Rodriguez (*The George Lopez Show*) and *Heart-Shaped Cookies* author David Rice (from nearby Edcouch, Texas) made a couple of independent films in Elsa, bringing into the local economy some much needed dollars. It almost didn't happen that way. Rice had been offered a lucrative Hollywood deal for one of the films, *Los Scavengers*, but turned it down when the producers wanted the movie to be shot in California. David's insistence on filming in his hometown cost him much money and many years of delay in making the movies, but I can't tell he regrets this at all. David loves where he is from, and since he steals the place's stories, he feels obligated to give something back. The author of two critically acclaimed short story collections and numerous other writings, Rice is largely self-taught and learned to write short stories by reading, re-reading, and painstakingly diagramming the stories in James Pickering's *Fiction 100*. He told me he got the crazy idea to write about Edcouch while he was living in, of all places, New York City. Walking across the Brooklyn Bridge one evening, it struck him that all the writers who had written about the storied bridge had done so simply because it was a bridge where they lived. Well, there were bridges where David Rice lived, too, and they were bridges that connected two countries and the lives of people on both sides of an international border. Why shouldn't he write about that? Weren't those bridges at least as important and interesting as the Brooklyn Bridge?

On a trip to visit my mother-in-law in Elsa, I saw David and Valente hard at work filming. It was a Sunday, and they had Third Street behind the HEB blocked off in front of a raspa (snowcone) stand. It was no small production. A large tractor trailer was filled with top-of-the-line Hollywood equipment. I'd met members of the crew the weekend before at a party at Isaac Guerra's house in McAllen. They were experienced Hollywood technicians temporarily out of work because of the tanking California economy now happily slumming it in south Texas working on two low-budget independent features.

Because of the movies being made, Edcouch-Elsans were, if momentarily, proud of where they lived, and this was because of two successful artists, Valente and David. All too often, though, people overlook how it is the artists in our communities who give us a sense of place. When *Gone Hollywood*, one of the two films Valente and David produced, was screened at Cine El Rey in McAllen recently, an older woman in the crowd rose to address the two producers during a Q and A session and said, "I've lived my whole life in Elsa, and until I saw your film, I never knew what a beautiful place it is. Thank you." I had a similar experience, years before, when I read a story by Rice that used the Globe department store in McAllen, Texas as a setting. I lived down the street from that store, and I never saw it—or the Valley—the same way again. An imaginative, literary representation had made my region real for me.

More often than not, though, regional artists encounter a different response: we envy them their success, ridicule their work as inaccurate or inauthentic, claim that we could have written the same thing, and in general still see them as the same people we knew in high school. Elsa is currently countering that trend. In Elsa, Valente's name is now on the water tower in ten foot letters. Rice, who didn't make it onto the water tower in Edcouch, might still have a raspa stand named for him some day—David Rice Ice. The best restaurant in town is owned by the Grammy-nominated Los Frijoles Romanticos. On the walls of the restaurant is a fine collection of historical photos of Elsa. The Romantic Beans know where they are from—and that's probably why their music is so good. See them for free or even jam with them on Thursday nights in the restaurant bar.

Edcouch-Elsa is midway between two other Valley towns of literary importance, Hargill and Mercedes.

Hargill is to this day barely a crossroads cut across rich, delta farmland. But it is the hometown of Gloria Anzaldúa, the author of *Borderlands* and one of the most influential Chicana writers and theorists of her time. She's not on the water tower in Hargill, though, and probably never will be. Back in May

2004 at her funeral (she died of complications related to diabetes at the age of 61 in her home in California), there were barely
fifty people present. The local newspapers in the Valley didn't
know who she was when she died, although in Austin, San Antonio, and San Francisco the newspapers ran full obituaries and
tributes. I was the only professor from a university in the region
who attended her funeral; my wife, David Rice, and Marissa
Taylor the only local writers to pay their respects. A fair number
of her friends in California, Austin, and San Antonio came,
though, traveling from major cities to a small fenced cemetery
where goats could be seen chewing grass just beyond the grave-
stones. At the rosary the day before the funeral, one of her niec-
es, who was in high school, spoke of having never met her Aunt
Gloria and of having only just discovered that her aunt was a
writer: her name was buried in a long list of possible research
paper topics assigned by her high school English teacher. The
young woman cried saying this, knowing she would now only
know her aunt through her work.

A few years before, a friend of mine had suggested that the
students in the Valley might do well performing some of Gloria's
poetry at UIL competition. The previous year, two students from
Edcouch-Elsa had placed first and second at State UIL competition performing stories by David Rice. It was the first time a
Mexican-American had ever won the state level competition.
Not surprisingly, they had done less well in previous years recit-
ing Poe and Updike. However, "Not that woman," my teacher
friend was told by the local UIL chair when Anzaldúa's works
were mentioned as possible performance pieces. "I knew her. I
know what she was."

What she "was" was a feminist and lesbian—that's all people
in the community needed to know—but she was also a poet, his-
torian, linguist, teacher, and community organizer. Her influence is immense. Six years after her death, there is already a
conference in its third year celebrating her work. Last year, as
part of the conference, more people came down on a bus from
San Antonio to visit her grave than were in attendance at her

funeral in 2004. They wanted to see where she was buried, but more so, where she was from. They knew the place itself was important.

The day before these visitors arrived, my wife went to the Hargill cemetery to clean Gloria's grave, a ceremony she has learned from her mother and grandmother. There were several snake skins on the grave, which she brushed away. For anyone who knows Anzaldúa's work, the snakeskins could be no accident. Erika ("La Erika") and two of her poet friends, Veronica Sandoval ("Lady Mariposa," who evolved from slam/street poet into a proud, bilingual Valley poet after reading Anzaldúa) and Lauren Espinoza ("Lauren Out Loud"), have been giving Anzaldúa-inspired readings for the past several years, billing themselves as The Trinity. Gloria's influence on them and other poetas has reached the point where her followers are semi-seriously being seen as a cult. This year at a UTSA conference, a woman from California who was a close friend of Anzaldúa and learned folk magic from her channeled Gloria's spirit and invoked it in a sage-smoke ring around participants' heads. "Gloria would be so happy to see you here, because you come from the Valley," she told my wife on Anzaldúa's behalf. That afternoon, Erika wrote a poem entitled "Crossroads," which she later found had eerie similarities to a poem she had never read by Anzaldúa. Anzaldúa conferences are as spiritual as they are academic, and Gloria (as we all familiarly call her) is on the fast track to becoming a folk saint. You can even buy Gloria votive candles, although they haven't made it into the HEB yet. We find this wonderful and amusing at the same time. In response, Lauren has written a satirical Catholic mass-style poem addressed to the Church of Gloria, entitled "Anzaldúaism: A Missal."

All three of these poets attended the same university from which Gloria graduated in January of 1968—the University of Texas Pan American. It has studiously ignored her presence for decades, although the past few years a speaker's series has been established in her honor and the UTSA conference includes a mini-conference in the Valley. In 2002, though, when the university celebrated its 75th anniversary, there was lots of money to bring a featured writer to the campus. Not surprisingly, Anzaldúa was overlooked, and instead a California writer, Gary Soto, who has no connection to the university, was flown in to the delight of the local public school teachers. Gloria wouldn't have been so welcome, I suspect. She wrote some nasty things about her alma mater, including how she had to take speech classes to rid herself of an accent. These speech classes were taught by white southerners who said "git" for "get" and of course had no accent at all.

The other writer besides Gloria who most deserved a venue at UTPA's 75th anniversary was Rolando Hinojosa, of Mercedes, Texas. Mercedes is a short distance south of Edcouch-Elsa, as Hargill is a short distance north. These are very different writers from different generations. In 1977 at UT Austin, where Hinojosa would teach a few years later, Anzaldúa's comp-lit PhD advisor told her she couldn't write about feminism and chicana writers because "Chicana literature was not a legitimate discipline," as Anzaldúa told Karen Ikas. In response, Anzaldúa left Texas for California, taking the ideas for her classic *Borderlands* with her. There in San Francisco she and Cherríe Moraga and others found yet more opposition, from white feminists, and wrote a book, *This Bridge Called My Back*, protesting the feminist color-line. Both writers, Hinojosa and Anzaldúa, spent most of their adult life away from the Valley, but their work is all about this place (even Hinojosa's fiction and poetry about the Korean War).

Hinojosa's most famous essay about his writing is in fact called "A Sense of Place," which he defines as follows:

> For the writer--this writer--a sense of place was not a matter of importance; it became essential. And so much so that my stories are not held together by the plot as much as by what the people who populate the stories say and how they say it, how they look at the world out

and the world in; and the works, then, become studies of perceptions and values and decisions reached by them because of those perceptions and values which in turn were fashioned and forged by the place and its history.

His practice as a writer very much follows this theory, so much so that I would say his works *in toto* (a dozen novels, plus a long poem) comprise the best and most comprehensive history of south Texas ever likely to be written.

Although Hinojosa fictionalizes the name of the county where his works are set (Belken) and of its main city (Klail City), quite transparently the real-life county is Hidalgo County and Klail City is Mercedes, Texas, Hinojosa's hometown. A year ago I taught a single author course on Hinojosa and in the spirit of discovering this relationship between his works and what he calls the "sense of place" I did the obvious and took my students on a field trip in their own backyard, Mercedes, Texas (about ten miles from the UTPA campus). Almost everywhere we went, my students had never been there before in spite of the fact that they grew up in the very region Hinojosa is writing about. Most of them were also completely unfamiliar with the history of the Valley that is in his books. Valley history is not taught in the public schools. Valley students know far, far more about the Civil War than they do about the Mexican Revolution, the Border Wars (1910-1918), or even the Mexican-American War, events much more important culturally to the region than was the Civil War. In their high school English classes they are more likely to be taught a novel about migrant farmworkers from Oklahoma, *The Grapes of Wrath*, than they are Tomás Rivera's . . . *y no se lo tragó la tierra/ . . . And the earth did not devour him*, set just up the river in the Winter Garden region. I can only wonder about the motives, if they are conscious, of Valley educators and school administrators who don't recognize the importance of teaching their students the history and culture of their region. What don't they want them to know?

I MEET MY STUDENTS AT THE HEB PARKING LOT ON TEXAS AVENUE in Mercedes. Across the street is a panadería, now on the site where Rolando Hinojosa's house once stood. It was a large, white wooden house, with beautiful gardens, and like all of the houses in the neighborhood, was a victim of urban renewal in the 1960's. My mother-in-law, Delia P. Garza (Hinojosa's neighbor and relative) remembers Hinojosa's mother, Carrie Smith, as being a beautiful woman with lovely blue eyes. Where the HEB stands, she told me, was a grocery store run by the Aguilar family. Across the street from the Hinojosas, lived the García family. One of the sons, Héctor P. García, went on to found the American GI Forum, the first modern civil rights group in South Texas. He and his sister were both medical doctors. My students are impressed enough to mark this hallowed spot where the Hinojosa house was with a group picture, but the main feature is a rusted green dumpster in the background.

We walk around the corner to Texas Avenue and headed south. It is one of about ten truly lovely days we have in the Valley, early November, temperatures in the 70's, a lively breeze, winter light. We pass the remains of the Rio Theater where Hinojosa remembers you paid five cents for admission and five cents for popcorn. The building is abandoned now. It used to show Spanish-language films from the Golden Age of Mexican Cinema; the other two theaters in the town, one of which has recently been renovated and restored, showed Hollywood films.

A few blocks south and about 6 miles from the Mexican border, the City is divided by railroad tracks. South is the Anglo part of town, which (as Hinojosa points out) the Anglos oddly called El Centro. Just before you get to the tracks on the left is the old brown brick police station, closed and boarded up, the wooden eves rotting. Hinojosa's father worked here as a policeman. There were three policemen; he was the only Mexican-American cop. In his novels Hinojosa creates a character very similar to his father, a Klail City policeman named Manuel Guzmán (Hinojosa's father's name was Manuel Guzmán Hinojosa). In *Klail City* (1976), Guzmán is contrasted with Texas

Rangers like George "Choche" Markham. Choche waves around a pistol, sticks his finger in your face when he talks to you, and perjures himself during the investigation of the murder of war hero Ambrosio Mora, shot down in front of the JC Penney's by Deputy Van Meers. By contrast, Guzmán just talks to people. No finger waving, no gun. When you have done something wrong, as Mora's father has when he tears down the plaque off of the war memorial in Klail City Park—protesting the exoneration of his son's killer— you simply turn yourself in to Manuel Guzmán because you know he will treat you fairly and with respect. George Markham, on the other hand, is likely to beat you to death. We film a student reading this story before the old jail house. A woman walks by and asks us, "Why are you standing in front of this old building?" "We're making a documentary about history," one of the students tells her. "Oh," she says. "That's good." And walks down *la ligne*, the railroad tracks dividing the town.

The Mercedes main street shows spotty health, every other building abandoned, windows coated in dust. The abandoned buildings make good places to put up "Go Tigers" posters rallying the local high school football team. One of my students, laughing I guess at the spirit of our field trip, says, "It's like we're on a European tour, but everything is ugly." We stop before the offices of the *Mercedes Enterprise*, publishing since 1908. A plaque tells us that the paper has chronicled the history of the Valley, faithfully and truly, since that time. Another student reads aloud a brief, fictional newspaper article from The *Klail City Enterprise News* in Hinojosa's first novel, *The Valley*. The newspaper reports on the murder of Ernesto Tamez by Beto Castaneda at the Aquí me quedo bar. It's a "south side" bar and a "hostess" is involved, says the *Enterprise* reporter. The brief story encodes practically every Anglo stereotype of Mexican-Americans: On the other side of the tracks, in the cantinas, every Mexican carries a knife, is violent when drinking, and there's always a prostitute involved. These "facts" may be correct on the surface, but the story Hinojosa then tells is far more complex—effectively deriding the idea that the newspaper tells the truth. It does tell a truth, but until recently Valley newspapers have always only told one truth—the Anglo view of it. Hinojosa, unlike the paper of record, recounts the story in depth from four points of view, based on interviews with the murderer, his sister, his brother in law, and the court transcripts (which make fun of the brother in law's broken English).

Two blocks down we stand before the First National Bank Building, a classical structure with columns supporting an architrave with the bank's name. It is now a ballroom. Perhaps this is where Jehu Malacara got his job as the first Mexican-American loan officer at the Klail City Bank. When "Ibby" Klail, finds out about Jehu's hiring, she asks the bank president if Jehu is going to be sitting out front where everyone can see him. No, she is assured, he'll be put out of sight in a back office. Jehu is so bewildered by the motivations behind hiring him that he disappears from his job (or perhaps it's because he's having a secret affair with the bank president's daughter). It's clear why he has been hired, though. The Anglos need a Mexican-American face to bring in the loans from Mexico and from the emerging Mexican-American middle class.

We leave El Centro and go back to Hidalgo Street where Hinojosa grew up and where Beto Castaneda lived. Mercedes had two elementary schools during the 1930's and 1940's, the North Ward School, which was exclusively Mexican-American, and the South Ward School, in El Centro, where the white children went to school. My mother in law told me that as she walked to school down Hidalgo Street to the North Ward School, you passed through the cantina district. Drunks would still be staggering out of the bars at 8 am, cantineras wobbling on high heels and laughing. North Ward has long been torn down and in its place stands a brand new elementary, John F. Kennedy. (There is no school named after Rolando Hinojosa nor is there any recognition of his place as Mercedes bard that I am aware of. Hinojosa was also the first Mexican-American hired to teach in the Mercedes high school; Cleotilde García, Héctor's sister, taught at North Ward before attending medical school in Galveston). On camera, a student performs a section of *The Valley*, John F. Kennedy in the background. Hinojosa remembers his first grade teacher at North Ward, an Anglo woman, constantly washing her hands in alcohol. Somehow, he says, they learned to read. In another story, the teacher asks a little Mexican-American girl what she has had for breakfast. The little girl lies to impress her (she has been reading a book about proper breakfast foods) and says she has eaten eggs, bacon, and toast. The teacher applauds her and asks another student what he has eaten for breakfast. Tortillas with LOTS of peanut butter he tells the class. In the integrated junior highs the Mexican American students of the 1940's start to fight for their rights against the Anglo kids. In one incident, the Mexican-American football players protest when they don't get their letter jackets, but in the end it doesn't matter—they die in the Korean War the next year.

In caravan, we take Texas Avenue back under the expressway and head West on the feeder to Mile 2 Road. Driving north, just a mile or so, it's already farmlands, tall sugar cane bending in the stiff west breeze. At Mile Nine road, we follow the signs to the Campacuas Cemetery. The cemetery is on a narrow two lane road bordered for a mile or so by tall waving palm trees and rows of orange trees ready for picking in another month or two. Rolando Hinojosa's father grew up here on the Campacuas Ranch, as did his father, and his grandfather. In his novels, it's Cano land, as it was in real life. The oldest marked grave in the cemetery is from 1877, Don Antonio Cano's grave. It's an above ground mausoleum with a pointed white monument on top. The cemetery has an air of very well maintained decay. A statue of the Virgin has been decapitated, making it somehow even *more* full of grace. A shattered stone cross has been reconstructed like a puzzle on the ground. Rough wooden crosses mark nameless graves. Still, most graves have flowers on them, plastic or fresh. My students are agog at the beauty of this place. I was, too, the first time I came here. Members of my wife's family are buried here. I took a picture of my children standing before their great great great grandparents' graves, who died nearly 100 years ago.

These ranches, like the Campacuas, are central to the counter-history Hinojosa's dozen books narrate. The Anglo story of the Valley is that it was largely unpopulated and certainly "undeveloped" (curious term land developer, Hinojosa says) until outsiders, "pioneers," brought their railroads, irrigation pumps, and banks to the raw south Texas frontier. The very orange groves surrounding the Campacuas Ranch cemetery, I tell my students, were impossible before this kind of "development." But what was here when ground was first broken on this cemetery where we were standing? It was a ranch stretching 9 miles south all the way to the Rio Bravo and fifteen miles further north: you couldn't ride it on horseback in a long day of hard riding. Many families lived on this and the other ranches for generations. Hinojosa calls this cemetery the Four Families Cemetery, and they still bury family members here. When I visited this cemetery with my mother-in-law on Dia de Los Muertos, there was an old couple sitting beside a tombstone who asked us, "Who are you?"—the blunt signature greeting of this clan. The man had, like Hinojosa's father, grown up at the Campacuas. He seemed uninterested when I mentioned one of his relatives is a famous south Texas writer.

I point to a distant windmill and some buildings and tell the students that on the other side of that levy is the Campacuas Lake. The valley is dotted by many such lakes, remnants of the Rio Grande when it was much wider, thousands of years ago. Up north you call these lakes ox-bow lakes; here they are resacas. The ranches almost all were based around one or more resacas. They functioned as a water tank for farming, the ranchers pulling the water out of the resacas to irrigate their fields. Trees grew close to the lake's edges making it a beautiful natural setting. For some reason the state of Texas claims there is only one natural lake in Texas, Lake Caddo in east Texas, but here in the Valley we have dozens. In this setting, for nearly two hundred years, families lived and thrived in interconnected communities. When the railroads and irrigation pumps and banks came in what Roma author Jovita Gonzalez called the anglo "invasion of the valley" in the early part of the twentieth century, this land was turned over almost overnight, through both legal and illegal means, to outsider Anglos. The Mexican Revolution in particular gave hungry land developers the excuse to accuse just about anyone who spoke Spanish of being a sedicioso, and soon their land was yours, and the "sedicioso" was your laborer on land he formerly owned.

This is what was called "land development." But the people here hardly needed it. You can see a glimpse of that self-sufficient un-developed past when you visit the Campacuas cemetery. And if you are curious about that name, you will find it is the bastardized name of an Indian tribe that used to live along this resaca before the Spanish—a reminder that while the Spanish might have been dispossessed of their lands by the Anglo invasion of the early twentieth century, they had done a pretty good job of doing the same thing to the indigenous people living here in the middle of the 18th century.

Again in caravan, the sun getting low, we head down highway 1015 almost all the way to the Mexican border to another ranch Hinojosa writes about. A small sign marks Toluca Ranch Road; you'll be in Mexico before you know it if you miss it. A couple of hundred yards south the sculptural, spiked "Border Wall" follows the contours of the Rio Grande like a perverted Cristo installation. It is a place that exists now only as a place between two other places.

Toluca Ranch Road is a rutted, dirty farm road—one lane—that tests the suspension on my 1995 Ford Explorer. About 200 yards down this road, to the right, is another narrow even more pitted road lined in towering palm trees and covered in their accumulated fallen fronds. About a hundred yards down this road, in the fading light, we see the old Toluca lake ranch house, a towering two story brick house with cupolas on the roof, a chimney on the side. My mother in law remembers relatives who lived here when she was a child in the 1940's, very formal

Spanish women who wore veils, had beautiful combs in their hair, and would laugh at their great-nieces' American-style hair, skirts, and blouses. They would arrive in Elsa to visit in a horse-drawn carriage.

A cloud of dust follows our train of cars up to this ranch house (it hasn't rained in months). We park before a low build-ing that used to be the general store for this area. The evening light that made the Campacuas Cemetery look so lovely has fad-ed a bit and makes this deserted place seem evil. The windows of the ranch house are boarded up or broken, the paint on the moldings long stripped by weather. The Ranch House, my stu-dents all agree, looks like a haunted house, and this place is in fact nocturnally visited by stoned high school students looking to spot a ghost (YouTube "Toluca Ranch" and you can see one of their videotaped nighttime trespassings).

There is the old general store, the house, and a much better preserved family chapel near a small cemetery. A state histori-cal marker is next to a "Stay Out—Private Property Sign." The marker tells the only story I have ever read about the Toluca Ranch, that is, other than Rolando Hinojosa's, and that's a story of how the Saenz family who owned this ranch on the Toluca Lake (another Resaca) were attacked by bandits in 1915 but their property was bravely defended by soldiers and Texas Rangers. Hinojosa tells a different story: that the property was not being defended by Rangers and the army, but was actually being attacked by them, and the family fought back. In Hino-josa's novels, the Buenrostros fight off the Rangers on the El Carmen Ranch when they try to force them out. In Hinojosa's novels, Julian Buenrostro crosses the river just south of the To-luca Ranch and kills the Mexican matones (assassins) who mur-dered his brother for his land. Hinojosa chooses to tell that sto-ry; official state historians choose to tell another.

Although the old ranch house has a Keep Out sign, and a low fence, one of my students (against my advice) walks over to the old house to inspect it, possessed, I suppose, by a spirit of historical research. Unwisely, she tries turning a knob on a back door. A hand on the other side twists the knob back. We hear her scream and see her running around the side of the house, yelling, "Someone's inside!" The house was not habitable by all appearances, but there is apparently a squatter inside. We are spooked and start to go back to our cars. From inside the house, we hear someone banging on the wood boarding up the second story window, not just banging, pounding, and a voice, in English, yelling, "GO AWAY! GO AWAY!"

In retrospect, it sounds to me like an admonition, a meaningful one. The places Hinojosa's work took us revealed stories that many might wish left untold. But we can't go away. It's our writers who don't let us.

Much of the material for this essay is drawn from personal interviews and experiences in the Valley. My mother-in-law, Delia P. Garza, was most generous in sharing her memories and, on our field trips, the backseat of my un-airconditioned car with my two small children. My friend David Rice knows my interest in biography and has told me many stories about his writing career. The references to Anzaldua all come from the second edition of *La Frontera/Borderlands* (Aunt Lute Books, 2001), which features the interview with Karen Ikas cited in the text. Information on Pan American College's 1960's-era "speech test" comes from Dr. Marian Monta, Professor Emerita, UTPA Communication Department. For the literary tour of Mercedes, I cite material from Rolando Hinojosa's novels *The Valley*, *Klail City*, and *Rites and Witnesses*. For biographical information about Hinojosa, other than information provided by his neighbor, my mother-in-law, I relied on a recently published essay that is very detailed about his hometown—his "Foreword" to *Héctor P. García: Everyday Rhetoric and Mexican American Civil Rights* (Carbondale: Southern Illinois University Press, 2006), pp. xi-xv. Erika Garza's poem "Crossroads" can be read on-line at *La Bloga;* her poem "Brown in the Wrong Town", published in *The Texas Observer*, appears on-line at texasobserver.org/poetry/brown-in-the-wrong-turn. Lauren Espinoza's work is published in *Time You Let Me In: Twenty-Five Poets Under Twenty Five* (Greenwood Books, 2010), ed. by Naomi Shihab Nye. Veronica Sandoval's work appears most recently in *Palabras en Vuelo: Words in Flight* (Tecolote Press, 2011) and can be read at www.facebook.com/ladymariposa.

Rob Johnson

Beneath the Encino

Manny stopped playing. He hadn't thrown out the trash. The grass wasn't cut. He was supposed to be in school. He strummed his guitar again, stared out past the drawn bed sheets his mother used as curtains. Waiting was like watching a plant grow.

The door opened. His mother. She was a stocky, heavyset woman in her sixties, wide and durable like any of her *bugambilias* along the front fence. She held a small, white paper bag. Manny struck a G chord, acted normal.

"What'd the doctor say?" he asked.

"What do you care, Emanuel?" his mother shot back. He could always tell when she was angry and at who. Her perfect Spanish included the full first name of her target in everything she said. "You weren't in your room, Emanuel. Jaime had to miss work to take me."

"I was in school," he said.

"*Claro que sí*, Emanuel. I'm sure that's where you were."

Manny felt he'd been pricked by a thorn all of a sudden. On the night before, he'd been on good terms with his mother, so much so that she'd even agreed to cook his favorite of all her Cuban dishes – *picadillo* on white rice and fried plantains. But it was clearer than ever now. Even she doubted him.

He looked down. His Yamaha Dreadnought was a shiny black, had a Rosewood fingerboard and bridge, used to belong to his brother when he played. There were fingerprints and smudges all around the sound hole. The jig is up, he thought, all of it. The getting up early and breakfast at Mickey D's and the two to three hours trying out the Les Pauls and Strats at the new Guitar Center on Ware Road before coming home for a bite with a textbook to avoid any questions – all of that was over.

"Where's Jaime?" he asked.

The glasses on his chubby-nosed mother magnified her tired eyes. "Outside. He wants to talk to you, too." She turned and disappeared into the hallway and Manny heard a door close.

He sighed and decided he'd face him like this: *Hey. Listen. Nah, just listen. I like delivering pizzas, all right? I like sitting in my car, driving around. And I like to reach into my pockets and the feel of crisp bills. College is four long years and I'm just not like you, smart. You got it? Good. Now leave me the hell alone!* That's what he'd tell Jaime. Finally. Once and for all. Come what may.

He took a deep breath, laid the guitar on the sofa. He peered out the window again and watched Jaime move under the arbor of the encino outside as a few small, green-gray leaves let go of their branches and spun down onto the grass. He realized it in an instant, the truth. Fall was on its way.

Manny hesitated, watched his brother a while longer. Jaime stood beneath the encino, his hair the same sheen of a well-washed black bean. He'd taken charge of things ever since their father's death a year earlier. Without Jaime, without his job at the university fixing computers, Manny knew: they'd have lost the house. What bothered him, though, was that he never heard the end of it from his mother with questions like *Why can't you just be like your brother?* or *Emanuel, don't you ever think about your future?* or his favorite question that never made much sense but which she asked anyways: *Don't you like girls?* His mother. No matter the occasion, no matter the company, she would always point out how Jaime dropped her off red car-pet-style in front of the Wal-Mart entrance before parking her Ford Taurus, or how her son mowed the lawn religiously on

Saturday mornings, washed dishes every other night, and fed the dog at seven o'clock on the dot. On top of that, Jaime even had a Mexican girlfriend and a college degree in computer information systems. *I dropped you on your head by accident when you were little, Emanuel. Maybe that's it?* Manny never answered, took it all in, ignored it as best he could, hoping it would go away. *And what do you think, Jaime? Why is your brother the way he is?* Manny watched the two of them discuss him as if he were an experiment they both had a stake in. *I don't know, Amá. I've got to go feed the dog.* Jaime's diplomatic answers made it clear as day for Manny: his brother would always be the perfect son in his mother's eyes; the one she could cling onto like fruit from a tree. *You and that stupid guitar. You never listen to anything I say, Emanuel.* He looked at his guitar and imagined the sound of a soft-strung E minor, the first chord Jaime had ever taught him, drifting off into the hum of ceiling fan above him.

Outside, the sun burned fierce outside of anything in the shade. Manny winced from incoming brightness. But he noticed something different about Jaime that day. His brother wore a rumpled brow, for instance, and hadn't shaved. His shirt hung untucked over an old pair of faded jeans. Jaime's entire appearance was as unkempt as the grass he walked on. He chewed on his fingernails, circled the encino, seemed to mumble to himself as a car hummed by.

Then Jaime stopped. He reached up with both hands and hung from a thick bough. Manny remembered planting that encino with their father years earlier, laughing and swinging from that same limb with his big brother through the years. It bothered him that he couldn't recall the last time they'd done it. He wished he'd written it down, the date, to have recorded the last time, then reminisce about it with Jaime. They'd been the same back then, it seemed to Manny. He wondered if Jaime remembered that now, hanging there in his black shirt and pants like one of those avocados their father used to steal from the grand tree in Doña Esperanza's backyard. They always fell with a thump, Manny remembered. Some even broke in half on impact. Everything inside was exposed.

A warm crunch greeted Manny's bare feet on the grass. The weeds brushed against his calves and knees, made them itch, all the way to where Jaime hung.

"Hey," he said.

"Hey," replied Jaime, looking down at his feet.

Manny wondered if it was all an act. It had to be. Jaime would boil over any minute, for sure. He was just biding his time. But Manny didn't feel like waiting any longer.

"I know," he started, his back feeling firm all of a sudden, his feet more grounded than ever before. "The goddamn grass is horrible! But I don't give a shit, all right? I'm not perfect like you!"

And Manny felt better than a rolling stone. Better than a slow jam composed of his favorite progression of guitar chords. Something inside him spread like roots, urged him on, transformed his newfound courage from a flimsy green to a thick-stalked, determined brown. His lips weren't quivering, and he liked the way he stood.

"I don't like school, and I forget things, to do things. I deliver pizzas, and that's who I am. Not you, okay? I'll never be like you, or what *Amá* wants. Never!"

And then he waited, realizing the music of his words had come to an end. But he felt ready nevertheless. Ready for whatever his brother might say.

Jaime didn't say a word.

Why wasn't he fuming? Manny couldn't understand it. Where was that strong temper of Jaime's, the one he'd inherited from their father? Where was that perfect storm always ready and willing to uproot Manny from anything he decided to do, call it stupid and childish, tell him it was time to grow up?

Nothing.

Blocks away, from the tracks on old Highway 83, a rare train whistled. Jaime finally lifted his eyes to Manny, and they looked frightened, like the last two raisins in their mother's rice pudding.

"Something wrong with *Amá*?" Manny asked.

"No, no. She's fine."

"Then, what?"

Jaime bore into the grass with the tip of his foot, over and over like some stubborn plow. As if he wanted to make a hole he planned to crawl into, Manny thought. The grass never gave, though.

Jaime stopped finally. He dropped from the branch, spoke as he fell into the shape of his bones.

"Ana's pregnant," he said. He brushed past Manny and went into the house.

Manny clenched his teeth. He stared at the encino and studied the thick, tire-tracked trunk, followed it from the bottom up, until the sun finally poked through the web of branches in a thousand bright pieces. He remembered when he was eight or nine, when the tree itself was young and thin, when he and Jaime fought over who could hold it inside the palm of his hand. Jaime always won in the beginning because he was older, his hand bigger. Eventually, Manny could do it, too, until the encino outgrew them both.

The train whistled one last time. Inside the house, Manny could hear his mother clamoring to God and the Virgin of Cobre as Jaime tried his best to explain. Manny surveyed he sea of grass all around him. To hell with it, he said. He made his way to the garage. He hoped the lawnmower had enough gas left in it for the entire job.

Robert Paul Moreira

Esta noche los muertos regresan

Era día de muertos, comenzaban los fríos de noviembre y las calles estaban grises, los edificios sucios, los ambulantes vendían calaveritas de azúcar llenas de moscas, me detuve a mirarlas, ninguna tenía el nombre que yo buscaba.

Entré al mercado y el olor a hierbas podridas hizo que me dieran ganas de taparme la nariz, mas no lo hice pues me intimidó la mirada hueca de una estatuilla: la Santa Muerte esplendorosa, rodeada de billetes, fotos y veladoras. Aquél pasillo pestilente era su templo, y aunque yo no creo en ella, tampoco quería que en el supuesto de que existiera, me castigara por hacerle un desaire.

Me acerque a un puesto de flores y compré unas de cempasúchil, cuyos tallos acomodé, como si se tratara de un florero, en el morral donde también cargaba un pan de muerto ya todo aplastado.

Salí del lugar y tomé un taxi. ¿Va hacer un altar, señorita?, me sacó plática el chofer, notando los pompones amarillos que emergían del morral. Le dije que sí. Me contó que el de su vecindad lo dedicaron a Cantinflas, y a la hija de un inquilino que violaron y mataron a la vuelta de su casa. En este pinche país nadie quiere quedarse sin hablar de las tragedias cotidianas, dije para mis adentros. De ahí se soltó con el sermón de la violencia, de los maleantes que manejan los burdeles, de la legalización de la marihuana.

Tonight the Dead Come Back

t was Day of the Dead in Mexico. The cold November weather was turning the streets gray, the buildings dirty. Street vendors hawked sugar skulls abuzz with flies. I stepped forward to look at them, but none had the name I wanted.

I entered the market, and the smells of putrid herbs made me want to cover my nose, but I didn't because the hollow eyes of a statue intimidated me: the Santa Muerte in all her splendor, Holy Mother Death, surrounded by bills, pictures and candles. That corridor was her temple and, although I don't believe in her, in the event that she existed, I didn't want her to punish me for snubbing her.

I approached a flower stall and bought some marigold, whose stems I settled—as if it were a vase—in my haversack, in which I was also carrying a squashed-up piece of *pan de muerto*.

I took a taxi cab and left the place. You will make an altar, miss? the driver asked, breaking the silence, noticing the yellow tassels emerging from my rucksack. I said yes. He told me that the one in his tenement house was dedicated to Cantinflas, as well as to the daughter of a tenant who was raped and killed around the corner from her apartment. In this goddamn country nobody wants to keep the daily tragedies for themselves, I said to myself. Then he started with a speech about violence, the thugs running the brothels, the legalization of marijuana.

Llegamos y oscurecía. Cuando bajé del auto ya traía mis llaves en la mano y la de mi casa preparada para abrir rápido, audaz, sin darle chance a los vecinos de observarme. Me pongo paranoica cuando se me hace de noche. Mi colonia no es de las peores, pero los asaltantes emergen hasta por debajo de las piedras. No me consta, es lo que cuenta la gente: los sicarios se llevan a las mujeres que les gustan, o te quitan el automóvil, o te matan porque les da la gana. Además, vivo cerca de una plaza y mi calle suele estar llena de pedigüeños, zombis haraposos y con rastras de mugre, llenos de enfermedades cutáneas; se acercan y hacen peticiones ininteligibles, que no pueden significar otra cosa más que les des dinero o comida.

Tras asegurar la puerta subí las escaleras del área común. Una rata yacía moribunda, ensangrentada, en una ratonera al principio del pasaje. Qué ironía morirse hoy, pensé.

Entré al departamento sin prender las luces, me detuve en el pasillo donde estaba mi altar casi listo. Encendí las velas. Acomodé el pan junto a las calaveras de azúcar, las cuales había ido coleccionando durante octubre y decían todas Rubén. Hice un camino con los pétalos del cempasúchil en dirección a la entrada. Serví dos caballitos de tequila, choqué el mío contra el vaso inmóvil y le di el trago sintiendo el amargor en la boca del estómago. Acomodé la fotografía de mi exnovio, con quien tenía más de un año sin hablar.

Te dije que para mí estás muerto, cabrón, musité en voz alta. Una onda de aire frío entró por la ventana y me apagó dos veladoras, las cuales volví a encender con la paciencia de quien no espera a nadie.

Me dio casi la media noche tomando la mitad de la botella, recordando a mi muerto vivo, quien seguramente estaría embriagándose como yo, en algún lugar de esta jodida ciudad, acompañado por no sé qué zorra, apartando más y más mi recuerdo, olvidándose de mi existencia.

En el fondo todo ese ritual grotesco —hacerle un altar verdadero a alguien que estaba muerto sólo metafóricamente—, lo

When we arrived it was already dark. I got out of the cab with the keys of my apartment in the hand, ready to open it fast, audaciously, without giving my neighbors any chance of watching me. I get paranoid when night falls. My neighborhood is not the worst, but robbers emerge even from under the stones. I don't really know it for certain, but it's what people say around here: the hit men take any woman they like, or they steal your car, or they kill you because they felt like. Besides, I live near a plaza, and my street is usually full of hobos, those ragged zombies with dreadlocks made of dirt and disease-ridden skin. They come and ask you for things in an unintelligible way that can't mean anything other than a scam for money or food.

After securing the door, I went upstairs. In the common area I saw a rat that lay dying, bleeding, in a trap at the beginning of the passage. How ironic to die on the Day of the Dead, I thought.

I entered the apartment without turning on the lights; I stopped in the hallway where my altar was almost ready. I lit the candles, put the bread between all the sugar skulls that I'd been collecting in October, all of which bore the name of Ruben. I made a path towards the entrance with the marigold petals. I served two glasses of tequila, took one in my hand and hit it against the other motionless glass. I knocked back the shot, feeling the bitterness spread throughout the pit of my stomach. Then I adjusted the picture of my ex-boyfriend, who I hadn't spoken to in more than a year.

I told you that you're dead to me, you bastard, I mused aloud. A wave of cold air came through the window and blew out two candles, which I turned to light again, with the patience of a person who waits for no one.

I stayed there almost until midnight, drinking half of the bottle, remembering my living dead man, the one who in that moment would be surely as drunk as me, somewhere in this goddamn city, along with some slut, putting my memory away even more, forgetting about my existence.

había tomado como último recurso para obligar al imbécil a que volviera.

Cuando el reloj de la cocina daba las doce, el sonido de un *toctoc* me sacudió. Debe ser que estoy borracha, porque yo no creo en estas pendejadas, me dije mientras iba a averiguar quién era.

El timbre sonó insistentemente, hasta que llegué a la puerta.

Rubén... masculllé entre los labios.

Pásale, te serví tequila.

Deep inside of me, all this grotesque ritual—making a true altar for someone who was only metaphorically dead—, was the last resort I had taken to force the idiot to come back to me.

When the clock in the kitchen struck midnight, the sound of a knock shook me. I must be crazy drunk, because I don't believe in this crap, I said while I went to see who was calling at the door.

The doorbell kept ringing insistently until I reached the entrance.

Ruben... I mumbled between my teeth. Come in. I served you a shot of tequila.

Erika Said Izaguirre

Jack Is Back

Long ago a clever thief named Jack tricked the Devil, trapping him until he agreed to make a deal: not to take Jack's soul to Hell when he died. Well, eventually the day of Jack's death came, but the guardians of Heaven refused to let him in since he had done so many bad things. Jack tried Hell, but the Devil reminded him of their deal. Jack realized that he would have to wander the world in darkness. The Devil felt a little sorry for him and gave him an ember from Hell that provided a light that would never go out. Jack carved a face into a turnip and placed the ember inside. From then on he has been known as Jack of the Lantern...

After long years of wandering, Jack of the Lantern has become bored. So he decides to play a trick on the Grim Reaper—Death.

"What if I made his scythe stop working?" Jack thinks. "I have a plan!"

Jack finds the Grim Reaper at a hospital, taking someone's soul. Tapping Death on the shoulder, Jack says, "Hey. I want to switch my turnip for a pumpkin. May I?"

The Grim Reaper, irritated, says, "Why are you asking me? Why don't you steal one like you steal everything else?"

"Okay, fine," Jack replies. He runs to a nearby pumpkin patch and picks a medium-sized one. When he returns, the Grim Reaper is still there. Lots of people are dying tonight.

"What do you want now?" Death demands. "Make it quick before I slice your head off like the Headless Horseman."

"Can I use your scythe to carve it?"

The Grim Reaper sighs. "If I lend it to you, will you leave me alone already? This job is depressing enough as it is. Do you have to make it annoying?"

"Okay, I promise."

When Jack is carving, he pulls out a little bag of salt and rubs it on the scythe.

"Here you go," he says, handing it back to Death. "Hee hee hee!"

"Oh, darn it, Jack!" the Grim Reaper yells. "Now it's useless. I can't take souls with a salted scythe!"

"I know," laughs Jack. "That's the point."

SO THE GRIM REAPER GOES TO HEAVEN TO GET A NEW STAFF AND TO Hell to get a new blade. The Devil and God give him the pieces, but they say he has to clean his mess up.

"What mess?" asks the Grim Reaper.

But that's the funny part, since two months on Earth is two minutes in Heaven and Hell. He gets back to Earth and finds Jack sitting on top of a building, shooting zombies with a slingshot.

"What the heck, Jack? There are zombies all over the freaking place!"

"Well, yeah. You see, all the souls are trapped in the bodies of the dead, so there's zombies. And you have to get every single little soul in the gigantic world...the ones that are trapped and the ones that are dying. Have fun!"

Jack laughs.

The Grim Reaper stares at him, infuriated. Finally, Death lifts his scythe. "Well, Jack, at least you carved yourself a pumpkin head. You'll be needing it."

Angelo Bowles

In Memory

No one really knows what happened. Only what the news reported. Only a few confirmed facts. How Jorge only lived a week past his twelfth birthday. Another crime in Weslaco.

Other facts. It was Jorge's first year of middle school. A future Central MS football player with helmet of hair, messy and curled, a dimpled chin, light brown eyes.

Best friends with his younger brother, TJ, three school grades below.

Played youth football with the Cowboys every Wednesday night. Buried in a purple football Panther jersey donated by the Weslaco varsity team, along with his favorite video games-- Madden '09, Viva Piñata, and B-K Nuts and Bolts.

I CAN'T STOP THINKING ABOUT JORGE'S LAST FRIDAY NIGHT. I IMAGine him at home with his mother and little brother, TJ, downing pepperoni pizza with generic lemon-lime soda, and loads of parmesan cheese. And laughing crazy when Nacho Libre stabs a man with a flying corn-on-the-cob on TV screen. TJ rolling on the ground in delirium and Jorge crying from laughing attack.

Friday nights, the ways my own two boys celebrate.

MY HUSBAND RECEIVED A CALL EARLY SATURDAY MORNING. HE WAS TJ's favorite 3rd grade teacher at Roosevelt Elementary and

Jorge's youth football coach for the past three years. The news was shocking, a jolt to the lungs. I had just spoken to their mother, Stephany, the weekend before about a team party. Even then, I didn't know the boys personally. Only that they were good boys, never late to school, always ready for football practice, never without their mom. What my husband has always said.

But the picture in the obituary tells me all I need to know. Jorge smiling and his mother kissing his cheek. TJ popping in on the right side, enclosing them in nine year old arms.

What haunts me most is what Jorge must have been thinking when the bell rang at the end of the school day. He must have thought the same as my son. My son who shared a table with Jorge in the 6th grade science wing every day right after lunch. TGIF and X-Box all night.

Until Jorge got sleepy. Until his mom said go to bed. At 11:00 PM. With his brother at the foot of the bed because he couldn't sleep. Because *el Cucuy* was in the shadows, and his mother was still cleaning the house, trying to get it ready for sleeping in tomorrow morning. What I think.

She'd already done enough work this past week. A sales clerk at JCPenny and a court appointed mentor to a six year old boy removed from his home. A case of neglect. Making a visit to the boy's foster home in Mercedes, town east of Weslaco, e-mailing, phoning relatives, teachers, anybody involved in his life. Channel 5 news reported.

Two bikes were found propped against the charred mesquite tree the next morning. At the edge of the embers dying on the front yard. Maybe ready for a bike ride to the park a couple blocks away from their house, blue wood-frame on concrete blocks. The old Harlon Block park off 6th and S. Bridge, where Jorge first played Pee Wee football at the age of six.

JORGE'S MOM, NEWS SPECULATED, WAS NO STRANGER TO ABUSE. Twice, dispatchers had been sent out to their home off Airport Dr. since late November, 2010, of the previous year. Domestic dispute with a man she had recently married. With the boys hiding behind cabinets, under the sink. Boys who did not belong to this man. A man who had been kicked out of her blue frame home one week before Jorge's twelfth birthday.

Probably Jorge's happiest week since November 2010. Maybe her happiest week with no one to tell her no anymore. No one to say she was worthless. Degrade her with words. Scare her with threats. No one to yell at her boys.

He was gone.

A BIRTHDAY AND ONE MORE WEEK PASSED BEFORE HIS RETURN. AT 1:00 in the morning. He was a horror scene, stealth with gasoline. While Jorge's mother showered because she had swept and polished and washed and mopped until she could no more. A close family friend said.

He did not wake the boys. He did not beat on her bedroom door. He doused the home and made fire in the kitchen right next to the family room with the X-box and the flat-screen. TJ sleeping restless on the sofa.

Then Jorge coughing a cough that would not stop. TJ worried for his brother and running to find his mother. She came out with a towel and hair dripping wet, her youngest son crying, saying Jorge's in trouble.

She tasted the crackle of fire, she breathed in the heat wrapped in smoke. Her towel fell to her feet, but she did not care. She grabbed TJ and forced him out the bathroom window at the rear of their home. Told him to wait by the street. Late October. The air dark. The lamp post burnt out.

He stood there on the front lawn alone, a 9 year old boy in a Scooby Doo t-shirt and no shoes, while the house raged, while his stepfather watched from across the street in a beat-up Ford truck, using a cell phone to call 911. He never meant that much harm—stepfather later reported to police.

Charred bodies found in the corner of the boys' bedroom. No clothe on Jorge's mother.

The final scene—Jorge crouched in the corner, no longer coughing. Head down, shoulders slumped, carbon monoxide all around. His mother shielding him, crying with him, praying with him, asking the Lord to protect them both, to look out for TJ, to keep the flames away, to enter heaven before the flames. Rocking her son like when he was three and crazy about Tonka trucks, a boy now bigger than her, one she knew was dying. One she could not drag through the fire, through the consumption of heat in the hallway. She had inhaled all the fumes. Desperate to reach him.

Minnie Vásquez

Valley Drawn

My how precious her smile as I glared into the screen of the singles website on the computer. She had long black hair and beautiful brown eyes that captured my heart in an instance. I was taken right then and there! At that specific moment, I knew that I would be with her; I knew that we would meet; I knew that we would be together and I knew that we would fall in love. How is it that the soul, the heart or the mind can predict such things? Is it a prediction? Or was it something that happened through a course of vigorous action on my part? Yet, it takes two to tango does it not?

We sent instant messages to each other and chatted which then led to the exchanging of phone numbers. The doors opened as we engaged in verbal conversation and intimate text messages along with pictures and short videos we sent to one another. We were 1500 miles away from each other but I felt her near me in my heart. How is this going to be possible? How will we meet and be together? These questions tested the very foundation and belief of "We are meant to be". Believing that destiny had finally presented itself before us we hung on to that hope. When two people are meant to be together it will happen.

I was in Chicago, Illinois, and she was in Edinburg, TX: I found myself having to continuously reassure her and encourage her about the truth and reality of a soul mate. Many people no longer believe in love or destiny. For many people things of this nature are merely a fairy tale or fantasy something that is told in stories to build a sort of creative empty hope. However, this is all true and real. She decided to come visit me so we could finally meet and all I could think to myself was "Is this really happening?" I sat at the airport waiting anxiously. I would look to the left, to the right, up, down and all around. I was a bobble head holding a dozen roses and she was nowhere to be found. My heart sank into my stomach as my head slouched into my shoulders and I was overwhelmed with sadness. All that I believed was gone from me as a vapor in the wind. I then heard a voice which said "Hey" and I looked up to this beautiful angelic face with teary eyes and my how precious her smile. My soul mate stood right before my very eyes and within our embrace, within our kiss and within our own breath; we found each other, we were everything we had been looking for.

Since then I visited the valley the following month for a few days. I went back to Illinois to finish up work and within a few months (which seemed like years) I moved to the valley and we were married. Life has been quite a roller coaster since then. I believe that God brought us together and God will keep us together as long as we are willing to cooperate with Him and do our part. I am truly grateful that I was Valley Drawn.

Rolando Villafuerte

Love behind Handlebars

I t seems like a long time, 1949. Measured by years, I suppose it is. But it doesn't hit you until you slow down, like a boxer in the corner waiting between rounds, you don't mind the blows until you see the mirror.

When we started migrating, it was not purely for economic reasons. There was turmoil in the family. Change had to happen. The experience of going up north had transformed us all. Somehow seeing how others live, even if limited to the role of invisible observers, made us no longer innocents. We now knew we could be doing something with our lives. Travel does that to you.

Mercedes for us would never be the same. Before we did not know we were poor. Now it was an ugly fact: we had to reach up just to touch the bottom.

Until then school had been paramount in my life. In the seventh grade, registering late, sometimes as much as a month or two, caused everything to double up. We had to keep up with our peers and find time to go back into the textbooks on our own to understand the fine points that were introduced during the time we were gone. The history, the background story of whatever was being currently discussed had passed for the rest of the class and we had to find it alone. Our studying, therefore, took on an intensity and seriousness greater than before. It became a job.

As I was investing more time in my studies, the yield was not even in proportion to the investment. My grades reflected a downward trend. Before seventh grade, I was an A student, never having to worry about study. Now my grades were low B's and C's. To further complicate matters, I was discovering girls-outside of my dreams. They were now wonderfully accessible. For the first time they responded by acknowledging my existence. Ah, pre- teen romance.

Andres Martinez lived just north of Hidalgo Street. Imitation brick siding was popular then-which was before asbestos was found clinging to the walls. The Martinezes represented a middle-class within the poor. That is to say, they were migrants but they had accumulated material things: a two-story home, and a new 1949 pea-green Dodge sedan decorated with a huge chrome ram on the hood, not to mention a truck or two.

Andres had a brand new bicycle. He also had a crush on Aurora Lerma.

Aurora had a best friend, Oralia Yanez. Oralia, to my seventh grade self, was a vision from heaven, *una virgencita* (a small Virgin Mary). Oralia was constantly on my mind.

We would bike over: first, past Aurora's house, then to Oralia's in hopes of catching a glimpse of them. Unlike the girls in the Mexican films, I don't remember them ever coming out in the evenings; I don't remember seeing them – other than in school and there they were always surrounded by bobby-soxers, their girl friends. There was no real opportunity to develop a relationship.

But that didn't stop us from hoping. It became ritual. School during the day, cruising on a bike in the evening while the sun went down. The "Tennessee Waltz" was the number one hit on the radio in the U.S. I didn't know it then but somewhere along the way, I had become bilingual and bicultural.

G.G. García

The Brown Paper Sack

The huge brown grocery sack, wrinkled as a baked potato, sat atop my first grade desk in thunderous celebration of its functionality, joined in chorus by my tidy braids and sturdy brown Oxfords. Craning my neck up and sideways, I just made out the teacher's curlicued brown hair knitted fiercely to her scalp and horn rimmed glasses that reflected the lids of other desks that did not hold clumsy paper bags, only neatly assembled Red Chief tablets, pencils and paste . Oh, those grocery sacks! When other girls toted Barbie lunch boxes or compact, specially-made lunch bags, we carried our bologna and mayonnaise sandwiches in monster sacks. Waste not, want not. The horrid sacks dogged us through elementary school.

It was 1960 and my first day of school, registration day at of E.J. Parsons Elementary School in Lubbock, a rectangle set upon parched yellow West Texas grass with two scraggly trees in front. I would learn the mysteries of the crisscrossed, circular and squiggly gray figures on pages that made my father wrinkle his forehead and laugh, "Ho, ho, ho!"

Gail, my third-grade sister, and I ate soggy Kellogg's Corn Flakes with sugar—Mommy wouldn't buy Coco Krispies and Sugar Frosted Flakes—and we donned the cherry-red corduroy jumpers she'd sewn for us, along with starchy white blouses with Peter Pan collars that sang out Clorox. While the twin two-year-olds and my little brother gobbled their own corn flakes,

Mommy combed my hair—nobly wrestling with "stubborn rats' nests," yanking my scalp so hard I yelped—and pulled, wrestled and wove it tight into two brown braids that hung obediently on each side. When she sprayed it with a film of Aqua Net against the escape of straggling hairs, it gleamed like plastic. Then she brushed bouncy bangs that curled under in the middle of my forehead. "There!" she admired her work. "You look like you came right out of Sears Catalogue!" She handed us each large sacks of school supplies. "Watch out for cars! Have a good morning!" she sang after she kissed us good-bye.

"We will! Bye, Mommy!" we chimed.

We walked, skipped and hopped along smooth, white squares, dappled with morning sunshine, furred with errant straggles of grass sticking out. Now we were both big girls. I was in school, while the twins and Doug had to stay home with Mommy. We carefully avoided walking on cracks. Something bad could happen, and it'd be our fault.

The principal guided us to the correct classrooms, and Ms. Vaughter, my first teacher ever, directed me to the correct seat. I sat rigid at my desk, waiting for instructions. Being good was my main talent. I preferred to be pretty, but my grandmother said, "Pretty is as pretty does," so, continually on the alert for opportunities to excel, I got an 'H,' for "highly satisfactory," each and every six weeks of elementary—well, except for the term when I sat next to Clark in Mrs. Walker's second grade. We talked and giggled, but that fun came to a sudden halt one day, with an abrupt, "Kathy, I want you to move to seat number two in the third row," and we never talked again.

I listened with ears perked up like a cat's and watched, too, for tight or quivering mouths or staring eyes, any sign of displeasure. My daddy was a teacher, and he knew I would be one of the smartest and best-behaved students. Busy Mommy had bought me all the right school supplies—I hoped.

"Children," intoned Mrs. Vaughter, "take out your Big Chief tablets." I reached into the bag, touching the soft, cottony paper of the tablet—it felt like toilet paper—and pulled it out of the bag. A stern Indian in a headdress, embossed in gold, stared ahead from its brick red cover. "Now open the lids of your desks, and place your tablets inside. Now quietly close the lid." I did just what she said. So did everybody else. I heard the whisper-soft closing of desks. Nobody slammed them.

"Now, children," she said, "find your big number #2 pencils." I felt for and grabbed the chubby pencils, painted bright yellow. "All right, now open your desks, and close the lids."

We did that, too. Out of the corners of my eyes, I saw equally tidy, quiet children dressed in yellows, oranges and reds, sitting erect in perfectly straight rows following Mrs. Vaughter's instructions precisely.

Ms. Vaughter continued in gentle, graceful song, like nursery rhymes—"Mary, Mary, quite contrary, how does your garden grow?"—until my brown paper bag was almost empty. Then she stopped.

But a wooden ruler, eager, sweet-smelling, polished and yellow, lined with a gold strip, rested in the bottom of my bag! She said nothing about the ruler! What should I do? Choices paraded in front of me: I could raise my hand and ask the teacher, but, no, someone might laugh. I could grab the ruler and slip it into the desk. But she didn't tell us to. "You didn't say Mother-May-I!" I imagined her saying, sternly. I could pretend there was no problem and leave the ruler there in the bag. But what if something happened to it? Mommy and Daddy bought it for me. Daddy worked hard teaching social studies to eighth-graders so he could buy things like rulers and the bread and milk and bologna and mayonnaise we would carry in those grocery bags.

Now Mrs. Vaughter was talking again. Maybe she'd tell us about the rulers! But, no, her rhythm changed. "Children, now that you have put up all your supplies, and the clock says 11:00, we are finished for the day since it is registration day. You may go. I will see you tomorrow, and you will begin learning to read, write and do arithmetic. Are there any questions?" Nobody spoke. Nobody even smiled. But she did. "Children, you may leave as I dismiss you by rows." She did so. "Good-bye, children. Watch out for cars on the way home."

Hundreds of locusts sang and flew around in my head, but I got up with everybody else, leaving my paper sack on the desk, and walked out of the room. Gail waited for me there, and we walked, without skipping and hopping, home. What would happen to my ruler?

"How was school today?" Mommy whispered, as she rocked a barely whimpering, almost sleeping twin. "Ready for some lunch?"

"It was fine," we said. Both our Barbies got married that afternoon, but mine got cancer and had to go to the hospital.

The next day, I filed in with the other neatly-pressed children to Room #23. The yellowy wooden desks, as clean and shiny as ice, were empty. My brown paper sack was gone. It had swallowed my ruler in its wrinkles and folds, and the janitor had thrown it away. My stomach became a tight, hard ball. I made the wrong choice. I should've known what to do.

Later on in the year, we needed rulers. "Why, Kathy, don't you have a ruler?" asked Mrs. Vaughter. Guilty, feeling stupid, I said, "I forgot. I'm sorry. I'll bring one tomorrow."

Kathy Trenfield Raines

Culebra

Her name was Elena, but no one ever called her that. No one referred to her as anything but "la vieja culebra," the old snake. She rattled like a tin can, errant cough escaping her lips mid-sentence. That is, if you could ever get her to talk to you. More often than not, she would stare at you with her cataract eyes, seeming to look almost through you. If she thought you were up to no good, she'd walk to the end of her fence; follow you along the sidewalk from her side, swaying slowly back and forth as she hissed at you. For the kids, it was a rite of passage. Could you walk the block with *la vieja culebra*? Would you chicken out like Pablo, make it to the gate, where you suspected she would jump out and grab you, piss your pants and run home in humiliation?

The neighbors started to wonder, when the weather turned cold, a dip to 76 in subtropical Peñitas, were she was. The neighbors chatted over fences, *viejitas* taking their time at the local pharmacy to catch up on the rumors about *la culebra*, trying to decide if she was dying or moving away, the *señora*'s stories were growing more and more fantastical with the passage of time. Señora Martínez believed that *la culebra* was dying, swore she saw *la Santísima Muerte* standing at *pobre* Elenita's doorway night before last, interrupted by a barking dog at the Zamoras house. Las señoritas Suárez, diehard romantics, were sure it was a long lost lover, come from Starr County to spirit her away.

They believed *la culebra* had spurned his love as a young woman and he had made it his life's mission to win her heart and he was now back to whisk her away to the lap of luxury.

One morning, the doors of the old house flew open, just as the *señoras* had gathered across the street to ask about Socorro's granddaughter and steal glances at *la culebra's* house. A young woman, a goddess of taut, tan skin slinked across the porch, curves hugged by a silky red sheaf. Purse, slung over her elbow, she sauntered down the sidewalk to the gate, walked through and turned to lock the past behind her. The house a mere husk now, *la culebra* shook her keys at the awestruck *señoras* and sashayed down the street in search of a new den.

Vanessa Brown

Their Reign Ends

Keeping distance for survival, we wait for their deaths with centuries old disdain. Hiding in holes from above and below, we observe the balding mammals waste their existence, destroying each other and everything else. Destroy to gain and repress to control is their nonsensical notion of life. Manmade pandemonium as blind dedication to their pointy temples, but not God. Annoyed at the brats He made, He is finally pushed to fulfill their careless requests for assisted suicide, leaving the anti-Christ without a purpose.

Climbing out of the ground and the trees, shielded from apocalyptic chaos, our patience is paid off by being freed from our minority status and rebuilt with the remains left behind. Once often tolerated for our squeaks and fluffy tails but mostly called vermin for taking up space in their excluded civilizations, we lived on as we looked out our windows, sockets of ivory skulls, as we claimed the world once more like our ancestors after the dinosaurs. Saluting the extinct species with little fingers aiming at the ground.

Diana Elizondo

Poetry Selections

Before

Before I commit my love to death
Hurry, let's try to beat the death wave
To the tip of eternal dreams
The world is about to end, they say
Predicted in the future,
History is never perfectly portrayed

Love me now, hurry
Before the end of the world sets sail on her canoe
Fluorescent pink and yellow hair
Bouncing off the reflection of death's sea
The end of the world is rushing this way,
Its paddle is tormenting death's breeze

Stiff and still,
Stand with me
While everything is suspended in time and space
Love me now if ever
To the beat of this disgrace

Melt me with your kiss
That draws a sudden dripping shadow on my back
Paused within old seconds
Leaving bulky trails
Obstacles that scar the present
A world that will soon cease to exist

Love me now, I tell you
I want to explode before the explosion
I want one more chance alive,
Material embodied passion
Love me now and spark the lightning
In these death black blotted skies

The black keeps approaching the sun
Quickly consuming our panorama
This grass becomes our hotel
Love me loud before we both vanish
Before I commit my love to death
Let's ignite this one last breath

Yaresy Salinas

Alive

Alive, connected
Skin fading, I'm alive
Submersed in the composition of obvious worlds deprived
Disguised within the naked eye
I am here, I'm alive

I'm as clear as the night sky
You blow smoke right through me
I'm a piece of sheer bold,
A flicker in a movie

My heavens

Atmospheric tiled floor
Lining the stranger's home upstairs
The stranger up there dances;
On his bare feet he prances
Down under the thunder,
The cause of my scare

We're alive, there's no doubt
There's something that connects us

I can hear your conversation in the distance
With someone who makes you act strange
We're connected

Through lines that link me to the floor
Through veins that fuel the universe
Through colors and motions that cartoon our worlds

We're here
We're involved
We're connected

We're here
We're alive in my soul

Yaresy Salinas

Like Flames on a Burning Man

I'll protect you
The killers will come to find only their face
A fierce reflection coming from the red of my warm embrace

I will fight for you
With the anger of a father about to kill his only son
I will defend every crater of your moon
I will ignite your neon sun

I'll be the tree of your branches
A sturdy home for your troubled youth
I will devour your phantoms
And make every season new

You jump off the cascade inside me
I dive up from underneath for a kiss
Patting down the sea foam that will catch you
I will tend to every bone, every bruise

I will be the one to survive you
I will inherit your only estate
I will bury you under the branches
And spend the days outside tending to your grave

Yaresy Salinas

Love in the Time of...

(for Daniel García Ordaz and Jan Seale)

Love in the time of
Yawning
Growing
Dying

Yawning
To swallow the humidity
Dying
To understand the simplicity

To swallow the humidity
Rocks turn to sand due to grief,
To understand the simplicity
The sea sends its tide quietly

Rocks turn to sand due to grief,
Due to the wailing mother's
The sea sends its tide quietly
To mute out the pain

Due to the wailing mother's
Love sits alone in a corner
To mute out the pain
Of lonely hearts' despair.

Love sits alone in a corner
Crying
Of lonely hearts' despair
Wishing

Crying
To the crowded heavens
Wishing
For love

Edward Vidaurre

Conversation with My Greñuda

What do I write for?

To make sense of how fast my daughter is growing
and how I'm slowing down.
She disappears into the blues, yellows, greens and tans
of the playground asking what the syringe on the floor
　　　is used for.

I tell her it's the sadness of what's left from last night's rain.
I tell her it's what's left of a fight between life and death.
I tell her
it's what's left.

She tells me
she thinks it's what keeps kids playing indoors,
building imaginary castles
and molding their future
with Play-Doh

though it makes no sense she made sense of it
evil lurks and if you're not right
wrong is magnified
leading you to the edge between reason and insanity

"Why is the playground empty?"she asks.
I say it's because kids don't know how to play

She says, "Or maybe parents need to be led by their hands
and not be afraid to get grass stains on their skinny jeans"
(there I knew she wasn't speaking of me).
I say it may be true;
she says, "I'm glad you're my dad."
I say, "I'm glad you love swings and slides."

She smiles.

Edward Vidaurre

Lorca in the Barrio

Travieso,
Chepe,
Lalo

the three of them frozen:
Travieso by the world of bullets;
Chepe by the world of syringes and acid trips;
Lalo by the marching of monks through his *barrio*.

Travieso,
Chepe,
Lalo

the three of them burned:
Travieso by the world of pigeon shit and chalk outlines;
Chepe by the world of drive by shootings and *rucas* with feathered hair;
Lalo by the world of banned literature and dead lecturers.

Travieso,
Chepe,
Lalo,

the three of them buried:
Travieso in Lupita's tattoo;
Chepe in the *carga* going through his bloodstream:
Lalo in the rooster's crow, the dog's howl, and the glossy eyes
of his *tecato* father.

Lalo,
Chepe,
Travieso,

the three in my hands were
three Zoot Suit scholars,
three crooked cops,
three birds of different races and autumn spirits
that flew around landing in blood stained sidewalks being

outlined by death.

Uno
y uno
y uno,

los tres enterrados,
con la ternura del Invierno,
con la tinta negra de palabras escritas antes del suicido
        de la primavera,
con las lágrimas de Sofía que espera ser realidad en el útero
        del verano,
por la miel que llora la Luna hace el triste mar en otoño.

Three
y dos
y uno,
I saw them run, hide and die
on the streets of Los Angeles
into a dark alley,
into the night of anxiety filled smog,
into the voiceless screams and anguish of their mother's
        open mouths.
into my sadness of domestic abuse and alcoholism,
into the bar with the velvet curtain,
into my own death unannounced last year.

I killed the last of the Chicano writers
and a few people in Arizona held their champagne flutes
        in the air.
While Menchita tucked in their little wonderful children
        to the tune of
La *llorona*, breathing over them.
Travieso,
Chepe,
Lalo.

Chicanas are hard,
but sometimes if you lay your head,
between their soft breasts you can hear the cries
        of a new generation
of *raza* with the knowledge and power to make a man shit

in fear,
y eso me conforma

Cuando ya no pude ver las luces de la ambulancia
pasando la loma sobre la calle Cesar Chávez
entendí que me asesinaron tambien a mí.
Esa noche en el barrio destaparon todas las sábanas blancas
buscándome entre las caras fallecidas, en las iglesias,
        los panteones,
callejones, y las aguas del rio frio.
Still they couldn't find me.
¿No pudieron?
No they couldn't.

Sin balas en mi cuete,
pero con un libro y lápiz en mi mano,
empecé a escribir poemas...

Edward Vidaurre

Not Welcome

i don't belong here,
i'm not one of them,

and they know it.

in the Rio Grande Valley of South Texas,
you're either brown,
or not welcome.

> *¡Viva la Raza*
> *Y muchas otras cosas!*

and
i say things like,
beg your pardon,
and
it's my pleasure.

they isolate me,
sometimes by mistake,
sometimes on purpose,
but always,

> *¡Ay! Mira a la Güera!*
mouth dripping with disgust,
at skin that won't tan.

the war is not in any cidudad,
it's in our backyards
it's in La Plaza Mall,
where,

Fresas, ¡bienvenidos!
Pinche gabachos cállense la boca!
Y, ¿Cual eres tú?

Soy una,
I am,
Es,
igual.

in Detroit,
there was no color,
people paid bills and worked
they don't care about you
your skin
your heritage
they just keep on walking,

in Chicago *también,*

pero aquí.

Aquí es el Valle del Rio Grande,

here it matters who had the land first,
here they still care,

here the wounds of social injustice still run deep.

i'd offer a band-aid,
but it wouldn't help.

Nina Medrano

Dos Amores (Two Loves)

Con el primero,	(with the first)

Firm and stong.
Grace unmatched
Honored
Loved
Revered
A force to be reckoned with.

Pero en el otro lado,   (But on the other side or other hand)
Mi otro corazón.   (my other heart)
Passion unchecked
Dream and hopes,
Collide.
No boundaries
No borders
No titles
No responsibilities.
I know him.
He knows me.

Mi otro amor.   (my other love)
To be with one
Makes me love the other more.
I could no more live with just one,
Than I could live without air.
There is no choice to make.

Yo tengo dos amores.   (I have two loves)
y una vida.   (and one life)
Sin with the other,
To be an angel with the one.
Fall with the other,

Not to break with the one.
Wrong with the other
Makes me right with the one.
They love me,
And I them.
Porque con dos amores,   (because with two loves)
Yo estoy completa.   (I am whole)

Nina Medrano

From the Valley

(sketches from memory 1979-1993)

I'm from the Valley of Southmost Texas
where there was a morning
children on their way to school
drowned in their school bus
in a water filled *caliche* pit—
Dr. Pepper Doom truck knockin' 'em to death
radio and TV told us to turn on
our headlights in mourning
not me though, too bothered by
the pointlessness of it to commiserate
that way and next time you see a school bus
look for the escape hatch on its roof
too little too late owed to those kids
dying in the sunless stagnant water . . .

Land of *colonias*
illegal shanty towns full of the unemployed
exodus from south of the *frontera*
land of the palm trees
and home of the grapefruit—what had *called*
the unemployed in those *colonias*—*las pizcas* of all sorts to
found--
of seasons past
since really are quite dead and gone
due to those freezes way back
when even our toilet froze in our crappy house in Sharyland

the land where most place names are white
yet the populace is of at least 90 percent Mexican origin . . .

The land of two *fronteras*
one to keep the Mexicans out or in
and one to keep us all in the Valley
Pues la Frontera en Falfurrias, '*mano, es pa que no salgas de
aqui* . . .

The place of five generation
pot dealers and single rolling papers
sold at convenience stores
for a dime plus tax

Of eighty dollar eight balls
30 dollar ounces of *mota*
Where floaters bobbed like corks
in the Edinburg Canal and *Rio Bravo* . . .

Home of the *corridos*
Where *conjuntos* played
accordions echoing in downtown McAllen
not far from Falcon Records
As transvestites dug in pockets
for passports
while blowing in beer soaked gloom of
hallways . . .

Where *los rinches* wore badges
lynching Mexicans
enforcing the hegemony
as paid to do
as Texas Rangers
providing fodder for yet more *corridos* . .

And in high school
Cholos with low riders
So-low-*vatos*
wearing *Dickie*'s

white wife beater under open short sleeve dress shirt
chains on display
way back before everything became just another
made by mtv identity sold by Pit Bull
singing while selling Dr. Pepper (there they are again)
diabetes in a bottle--
So much for *la Raza*, no?
But he's some Florida Hispanic
nada que ver con el Valle—
no es hijo de la frontera . . .

Where English is a hybrid
Spanish too, and antiquated words
trapped by *dos fronteras* away from
La Real Academia Española
still had life-- *nadien* and not *nadie* was the norm
and *asina* was how it was done . . .

Where the industrial smell of Reynosa
and *maquildora* bruise over its sky
knowing no borders
easily comes to visit . . .

Where in my Chicano Literature class
at old Pan American right after UT took it over
a woman said she hated "white" Mexicans
because they could
go back and forth
between worlds—
Being one, I said *chingado*
to *her* racist brown self
but then again in the right conditions
I can be as she
and being brown has nothing to do with it in the end;
can't escape your blood . . .

And la *isla del Padre*
where stolen by Spanish gold
washes on shore
and if you find a *moneda*
cállate el hocico
porque the Spanish are going to want it back—
the flag and all—
they think what they stole is theirs not thinking to give it back
to whom it was stolen from, or finders keepers,
losers weepers . . .

Where the rock station KRIX 99.5
Rocks the Valley
played "The End" by the Doors over and over after it
was bought out
waiting to go off the air
before being replaced by a *tejano* station . . .

And the place where *mi papá*
nació;
San Juan
Home of the Shrine to the Virgin
where my *abuelos*
had followed the call and been working
las pizcas when my father demanded
entry to *el Valle* not knowing where he was--
And after his birth they
were kicked back to the rancho outside of Monterrey
but he was a citizen by birth
and that is why I am writing this in *mostly* English--
Why the Valley was home for so long . . .

It's the place
donde dos vistas cross invisible lines
and a visible river
coming into, *a veces,* a blurry view
compartiendo
the best and worst of themselves
and everything else . . .

Juventino Manzano

Driving Home from Kingsville

The ink is scrawled across the page,
haphazardly in manic madness
it read, "Gone home,"
and so I left it, there on your nightstand
as I planned my final farewell.
Hop on the bus, morning ride
back home to the Valley
before a more sober head
changes my mind to stay instead.
You will learn to find,
I was up past dawn,
the reason? Nothing special,
nothing that matters anymore,
the final hints of backwoods music
long since past ringing in that clouded mess
between my ears. It was realizing,
me realizing, I realizing that
you'd be everything you wanted to be,
and me? I'd be everything
you
wanted me to be.
Rum soaked logic, the type that runs
its cruel curse through your words
that chastise,
reganize
recognize
who we are and where we strayed from.
I found these answers last night
driving in from the coast,
past silhouetted mesquite, two dark lanes blurred
in the booze of a wild night of dancing
that a lonely *lechuza* howled
its delightful approval of.

And there
in the moonlight, like an oasis a dried up gas station can be,
a full view of velvet blankets swaying hauntingly
revealing *fotos y recuerdos* of *La Santa Virgen* or
Selena, something in the way they hung
on tattered clothespins--rephrase--
orquillas my love in case you forgot words like this once existed.
Sí las tengo in my lingo but how they burn
if I fail to read them with *ganas*.
They might as well fall on the ears of the deaf
as they did when I noticed you passed
out in the lap of some drunk hick in the back seat
that once was your love and mine.
With this in mind, pulling in to some
South *Tejanista* town some King rancher claimed as his own
once upon a time. Blankets,
they just as well represent my corazon on sale for twelve bucks
or two for ten if I had one to spare. To wit,
or *ahí tu y tus pinches palabras* a third year college course
at the university got you...
We return you now to your regularly scheduled bs
which is meant to mean something
to me
for me
against me
but it's alright long lost lover
karma's a bitch that keeps on giving
and that full moon that night only fed
the process of my returning to *mi mundo*
full of mass rituals, lighting candles
burning incense
while reading a tattered *baraja de tarot*.
Bad news isn't always bad. *Sigue*
mi corazon
despite
in spite

with it's own right
to seek all knowledge, verdades
beyond the bullshit that fits neatly between your ears.
Chew on that my blind little coconut
and see you in the next life
should we consider ourselves slaves to the bad luck truck.

Héctor Gómez

Tejanese Wisdom & Twisted Logic

Espero
que me mandes tu sonrisa
or a wink across this internet stratosphere
inner sphere
como si fueran los fines del mundo.
The last vestiges
of human messages
across this static channel is the only way
to smell that sweet scent you left behind
in the backseat of our youth
where and when we'd unwind
entwined
to the tune of too much tequila.
Which ruined the way we made love
but only because we could not
remember our names much less
remember which hand touches which
or which way goes this or that.
You laughed, you made sense.
You only laughed when you made sense
of it all. Enough to say so seductively,
"*Ay, mi vato, mi ese, mi mundo.*
We can't love each other forever.
Te mandaré a la chingada"?
Forget we were ever here, mi amor.
Hope only exists for us
in the safety of our selfish pride and ways.
Then maybe,
someday *te mandaré*
a little smile, a wink
across an endless frontier.
"*¿Cómo la vez?*"
And I think,

¿Serás tan gacha con mis esperanzas?
Or do you forget
how most things passed us by
when we believed time would
last forever. And all our wasted
chances came from an infinite deck of tarot.
Como si fueramos tan inocentes con el amor
in the backseat of our youth.
Is it the sound of my name from your lips,
or the twisted logic of my tejanese wisdom
that still makes me love you so.
To wit,
to wait, and wait forever only wakes
some hopeless illusion for the sake
of a tattooed memory
donde existen amores
too haunting to forget
and to painful to forgive.

Héctor Gómez

Of Want to See You

Dreamed of you,
at a distance.
Found it sad,
we had
nothing to say, but...
"hello."
Uncomfortable silence.
What happened, my dear muse?
When a smile from you
was enough to remind my cold heart
that God grants you a day,
He doesn't--
promise them?
My mind, twisted,
confused,
thoughts so ego-infused
that I took so much for granted
felt our love was so planted
and only seeing you would be the least
of which we would do
to rekindle something I felt would last
forever.

Héctor Gómez

Concrete Smiles

The T.V. entertained empty couches
Most of the day till the sun fell
Fast asleep

The kitchen tables hold stories
Of homemade oatmeal,
 Peanut butter cookies
And *tamales*
Thanksgiving turkey and stuffing
And that one project
We all had;
Glitter and glue

The never ending gambling
Between siblings
Playing *Lotería*
For pennies and nickels
Coca–Cola bottle caps
And beans for place makers

The old beige telephone
Next to the beige coffee machine
Called my friends and *primos*
And spoke to them
About meaningless things
In only thirty minutes
Because that's how much you got
If you were punished

The bedroom whispered
Secrets my sisters and I
"Only" knew
Though I think Ma had more ears

Than two

El Cucuy
Fed on my misbehavior
And slept
Underneath my squeaky bed
While I used
My hand-me-down covers
With a fierce grizzly
As a metal shield

The kitchen walls
Can tell you
Endless conversations
Between Ma
And everyone who has ever walked
Into our home
And tell you
About the family meetings
When my sisters and I
Disobeyed

The *comal* laughs at me
From the first time
Ma asked me to check if it was hot
My hand still tingles

The soccer ball remains deflating
In the corner of the garage
From all the years kicking it
Back and forth to Dad
In elementary and middle school
Our tummies laugh
From that one time
Dad's powerful kick
Steered the ball

Straight to my face
He hugged me
When I cried

The attic
Filled with the grey sea
Of dust
Is now packed
With our plastic houses and dolls
That will always
Permanently showcase
Their concrete smiles

Valeria Espinoza

the fast lane

a blanket of darkness gradually tucked in South Texas
  as i drove home from his place in Donna
   a thirty minute drive

    i glanced at the radio
     track 13
      my favorite
       the acoustic guitar accompanying Hailey Williams
        singing mellifluously

        a sting from my earring made me gasp
         the heater was too high

          holding the wheel
           i turned and glanced at the digital clock
            dreading the long drive
             twenty more minutes
              i could count the cars on that highway
               with my fingers
                it was colder now
                 as the heat walked away
                  hand in hand with the sun

                  i peeked in the rear view mirror
                 six incandescent lights
                three vehicles
               coming from behind me
              passing me
             faster than a click of a pen
            my eyes were caught in the action
           a mustang
          a truck
         an suv

behind the wheels
adolescents

i continued at 70
in the far right lane
when the mustang lost control

the truck
the suv
  stopped half a mile ahead
  both drivers rushing out
    leaving their doors open

      i no longer saw that mustang
        i kept driving
        ignoring
          the acoustic guitar playing
          the heater
            the other vehicles
            as my eyes focused
              on the mustang
                the truck
                the suv
                    my contacts dried up
                    i forgot to blink

                  whose idea was it
                    to race on Expressway 83
                      assume it's okay to
                        allow young juveniles to drive
                        past their bed time, to think

                        no ambulance would be needed
                        to terrify innocent civilians
                          trying to get home to their
                          families

my friends tell me they speed
because the adrenaline rush
gets them as they press
the gas
because they're bored
for pride
mustangs were meant for speed
one said
for money
they could use the extra cash
on things
they absolutely don't need
if Vin Diesel can do it so can they
it's called an EXPRESSway
not SLOWway

images of family members
weeping for their ignorant child
crammed my mind
as i struggled
to comprehend the purpose
of this game
in the fast lane

McAllen, TX,
  thirty minutes have passed
  finally home
  it was a lot colder now
    the smell of Season All
    being sprinkled
      on a fish fillet
      occupied my mind
      and for a moment
        the mustang was forgotten
        until i turned on
          the television hours later
          "Channel 5 News Breaking Story...
          two men killed today in a car
          accident on Expressway 83"

Valeria Espinoza

Going to the Yonque

I'm going to the *yonque*
to buy me a satellite
Gonna pay the man five dollars.

He says he wants Incan gold
I tell him I'm not Incan
He says fine I'll take Mayan silver
I'm not Mayan
He says fine I'll take whatever you got
I hand him a note that says I owe you five dollars
He says, this ain't worth nothing
It's just a piece of paper.
I say, he has my word that the paper is worth five dollars.
He says do you have anything of value
for collateral, he says
I tell him that note is my collateral
It's my word
He's says, no, *güey*
Your word isn't good enough.
What if I give you some of my land?
He asks me for the deed
I give him another note that says I am giving him some land
He says, this ain't no deed
this is just a piece of paper
Sure it is
I point to the top of the paper
I clearly spelled it right "D-E-E-D"
He says that ain't official
Why not?

He says, well, because it ain't typed.
I pull out another sheet and this one's typed
He says, this ain't no deed either.
I say why not, it's typed out
He tells me it's a poem
I say that is my deed to my land
He says, you can't buy nothin' with a poem
I say, but it's typed
It don't matter
it's just words
I tell him that this poem was written by my great-great-great-
grandmother's brother
and it's worth more than
Incan gold
Mayan silver
or five dollars.
Well, was he famous? he asks.
His name is long forgotten
but his words live on like a tune
you can't get out of your head
it whistles in the wind
and splashes on the shore
it bakes in the sun and crackles
to a rhythm that thumps in my chest.
It lives in the heart, it lives in the blood
My heart? he asks, My blood?
Yes, in blood and words.
He says, What do you want with that satellite anyway?
I'm going to fix that old piece of junk
and launch it back into space
loaded with this poem
so that the world will hear it from cell phone tower to cell phone
tower.

He says, Fine, but I'm not gonna sell you that satellite
I'm gonna give it to you free and clear
but you got to promise
that you send that five dollars
up in that satellite with that there poem,
so that the whole world knows,

>   this poem ain't for sale.

Christopher Carmona

Roads

ROADS like numbers that never end
even when they end
my life spent on that asphalt ground
burning the bottom of my soul
with reflected heat from Rio Grande rays
they scorch only my edges
and keep me rolling like stones
that gather no roots.

so many ROADS to travel
too many miles to count
too many rotations of tires that are gradually wearing down
like the tips of fingers that have picked cotton all their life
and have nothing left except calluses
and thousands of bales of cotton
so I drive down ROADS in my cars
the wind and the radio my constant companions.

the history of me is the history of ROADS
my roads 281...83....I-35...Hwy 100...77...and 45
I know them well like I know that
left-handed hummingbirds cannot be trusted
and the typewriter is holy because it is bulletproof
once the keys have struck ribbon the ink bleeds ideas
          onto blank pulp
I know these ROADS even when they are covered
          with flashy orange cones
and guarded by black cruisers making sure that I am not
          one fast move
from the end of my voyage.
I know these ROADS because I am constant like the pyramids
          in Mexico

These ROADS are my ROADS because even when they end
        they never really end.
I am a traveller trying to perfect his drive
but I can never have find that perfect balance
on that perfect ROAD because I exist in transit
never wanting to arrive
never wanting to experience stillness
never wanting to forget the feeling of these ROADS
because then I would stop and maybe
just maybe I wouldn't be able to start again.

Christopher Carmona

Amerika

I dreamed a dreamed last night
of AMERIKA sitting on the tailgate
of a '79 black Camino that I never owned
she had cotton-candy hair and a short
mini-skirt that glimmered in the sunlight when she crossed her legs and rocked
her bare foot back and forth nervously
she bit down with sugar rotted teeth
on a pencil made from West Virginia coal-
miners and disappearing rubber trees that
that are now deep-fried strip malls.

She was scribbling away on her Big Chief notebook
made from real Indians and writing TV shaped words
that only appeared for $8.99 a month debited directly from
beneath Grandma's mattresses or from that old Folgers coffee
can on top of the refrigerator that was once made in AMERIKA.

The words she writes are not about me
they are never about me
because I
am a story
she cannot bare telling.
So she takes that big eraser
and tries to erase me.

First, I feel my arms and legs begin to fade
like that picture that Marty McFly
always carried around in Back To The Future.
Then my legs, so I can't run away.
I believe it is over...forgotten like polaroids and rotary phones

But then something happens...
her eraser won't work anymore
she tries over and over again
but it won't work...it seems I am written in ink...
she looks at me with arsenic in her eyes
and I look back at her and smile...

Christopher Carmona

A Flower

She smiles in the sunlight
Glimmering leaves intensely shine
But alas the dark doth come to lull down the dim-lit land
Shivering in the shadows her petals fade to grey
Like the day, 'twas sweet to part with her, a flower
A kiss a thousand-odd miles away.

Words

We read the words that others share.
Perhaps to help us get somewhere.
Yet as we read in to the words our thoughts
      in accordance do flow
Deeper and deeper we introspectively go.
Where our thoughts and words take us...
We pray no one knows.

Leopoldo Farías

Lange Memori

De trans la River'
la dolĉaj uvoy nigraj
el la plej suda sudo:
Ĉilio.
En mian kapon releviĝas
oblikva stelkruco
kontraŭ la noktveluro
de hemsfer' alia.
Interas dezertoj, ĝangalo, montoj
kaj multidiome popolo post popolo.
Orienten de tio rekonturiĝas
el antaŭa vivo
la Kabo amata,
kun muskataj uvoj eĉ pli delicaj.
Ho memorita gusto
kaj enmiksiĝ' amara
de lasta adiaŭ!
Larmoj en la Riveron.

2012.02.16, Edinburg, Teksaso

Original Esperanto version.

Edwin de Kock

The Tongue Remembers

From beyond the River
the sweet black grapes
of the most southern south:
Chile.
Into my head again
obliquely a starry cross arises
against the velvet night
from another hemisphere.
In between lie deserts, jungle, mountains
and many-languaged people after people.
East of that once more the contrours
from a previous life:
the beloved Cape
and even more delicious Muscat grapes.
O remembered taste
and bitter admixture
of a last goodbye!
Tears into the River

Edinburg, 2012.02.16

English translation by the author.

Edwin de Kock

The Queen Palm

Trapped in a tower's naked trunk,
the queen palm hears the call
of spring:

let down your hair...

She unfolds a golden
cascade of kernels
from her crown of fronds,
dangles petal clusters
for pollen to grip and climb.
The flowers tangle in the wind
like bed sheets, underneath
the legs of lovers.

Soon, pods ripen into dates
as summer passes through –
an orange bouquet of blush.
The end of cicada songs click
like steed hooves atop cobblestone.

Branches, tired of heaving
seeds, unfetter them
to the wild bed of crabgrass
and clovers. With a thump,
the seeds sink into earth, germinate

and root into the next generation
that begins like a fairy tale,
with *once upon a time.*

Katherine Hoerth

Summer Song

I.

A song of heat resounds across the brush
of Rio Grande—lullabies of sun
to seedlings nourished by the rains of spring.

To us, the idle—those who spent their dusks
unsoiled, this season sings a drought dirge, turns
our yard to desert. Nothing blooms - no sprout

of phlox—no hue to bring the hummingbirds,
those buff and iridescent shots to blush
in summer's empty sky.

II.

We wanted flora when we heard the hum
of honey bees, the laughs of kiskadees
devouring citrus back behind the fence.

It's late July and now you want to watch
our buds unwrap, to guess the hues before
they open like an infant's eyelid. Spade

in hand, you start to carve our russet earth.
You bring a marble bath for sparrows, haul
in trellises for when the jasmines crawl.

III.

The sprinklers click, but daylight dries the blades
before the roots can suckle. Together
we spread chemicals all across the lawn

for earth to swallow down as hoses run
through sunny afternoons. The song of heat
persists, but we can't hear it rustling

the drying fronds, or feel sweat dripping down
from forehead down to cheek. We dig through heat,
through August. Darkness comes; we sit beneath

encino shade. You kiss my forehead, hold
me close and whisper: *Soon, tomorrow, the earth*
will ripen beneath our boots.

Katherine Hoerth

Chocolate Sundae

I didn't mind the way our fingers
Interlocked to create a sundae, vanilla
with a little hot mocha drizzled on top.

You didn't mind me calling you Johnny
instead of Juanito, and I didn't care
that you couldn't even say my last
name.

I didn't mind when you came to my door,
and my dad sized you up with his blue eyes
and ordered me home a little early.

Or the way your mom ran her dark
fingers through my blonde hair, dreaming
of fluffy white haired babies. I didn't mind biting

into the corn husks that held tight
the homemade tamales, and you didn't laugh,
except maybe silently to yourself.

But when you took me to Denny's
one sparkly night, we sat cozy together
like teenagers do. I ordered like a fool –
a veggie burger please with those curly fries
And a sundae – with tasty hot chocolate sauce.

You just stared at your lap and said nothing
for you, just maybe a coke.

You watched me eat my fill, swirling
the ice cream together as it melted
into a single colored slop, leaving much
on my plate. You took the bill
into your trembling hands, emptied
your wallet onto the table, and we left
Arm in arm, you – hungry yet content,
me – full and yearning for something more.

Katherine Hoerth

Al Menudo

Menudo, tamales, mole, chiles rellenos,
will not be eaten by the children.
"Why?" you ask, but should you ask?
Look down, fool. Look at your plate.
What do you see?
What do you eat for breakfast, lunch, and dinner?
Pancakes from Denny's?
Eggrolls from Jack-in-the-Box?
Taco Bell?

If a cheeseburger is what they see you eat,
that is what they will eat,
and what your grandchildren will eat.
Don't be sad.
Don't be disappointed in your children.
They are not at fault.
If you want to preach "culture,"
be culture...
al menudo.

Sylvia Pérez

Fueled

I used to fueled by politics
fueled by ignorance
injustice
one sided arguments
incorrect rhetoric
holes in the logic

I used to be fueled by my hatred of hatred.

Used to love to argue with my father.
So much time wasted on issues that would never be resolved
which will never be resolved
and are fueling politics, ignorance, injustice, rhetoric, hatred.

(Borders close, eyes close
our hearts close and we remain
oblivious)

But I *used* to be fueled by all this.

Now I meditate on the altocirrus
listen to the wind in the cotton wood
sound like rain on a sunny day
walk on the leaves, our winter's autumn,
run after a three year who is fueled with life
with curiosity, with eternity.
I listen to the wind chimes in the live oak
and watch the vultures circle palm trees,
roost, kiss.
I watch as children balance on curbs,
try not to lose my patience.

I used to be fueled by my hatred of hatred.

Now I know only love of love
and how love
can silence
even screaming politicians
how it makes them lose their
composure and cry.

I used to be one sided
now my love is infinite
The sky isn't the limit.
And heaven is a 3 year old who needs me to help her
Hang from a monkey bar
Because moments like that do, last forever.

Erika Garza

Río Grande

how do you steal your own memory
mimic your own voice
write something
without
writing
about it

"*Pues esas cosas no se dicen*"
I've been told.

so I've sealed my own heart away
and
sent it to *silencio*
ripped my hands off
erased my face and
drowned my past in the
Río Grande.
I cross it back
this cross on my back
and deny myself the freedom.
to dance
because
I have forgotten rhythm
so clumsily I fall
back in to the
Rio Grande
and wet,
have gone home to
black out pictures
so no one knows my ancestors.

Erika Garza

Curar

Folk cures in our memories
ailments like *empacho*
cuando te estiran el espinazo
dislodging unbaked biscuits and
undercooked pancakes
while lying on your belly staring at the gray carpet.

Or barridas from strange ladies
whispering prayers and whipping rough branches
on all the corners of our feverish bodies.
Drinking teas from bitter herbs with bitter names
or dark rooms in homes we do not recall.

Was it *susto* from seeing the trenchcoat man who
slept in the Rotel tomatoes cannery
that went bankrupt sometime in the 80's?
Black moths that bring death to yellow Chevys?
Car wrecks on the Sunshine Strip?

Endiabablas repeating mamadas
that we thought satanic.
What *espiritú* on the breeze impaired us
leaving us mute?

These *barridas* only frightened us further
more so than before we watched the
spring break murders,
narcosatanico sacrifices on the *tele*
hoof and chicken claw
or the Llorona
that we heard call us in the
gallinero gloaming.

The only cure we ever thought did any good
was the cold egg our gentle mother would
use to pray over us
then break into a glass.

Or the *té de limon* Dad would make from lime leaves
To take away our sore throat.

Erika Garza

Perspectivas

En azul gris,
se tornasola la tarde.

Su basáltico a plenitud
asedia el agua marina
—aguamarina apacible—.

Tornasola el fluir
de la consciencia:
azul gris,
tarde en fuga,
asechanza de la noche
con su telescopio audaz.

Don Carlos, ¿cuál es
      el astro verdiazul
         de la memoria?

Juan Antonio González

Perspectives

In blue-gray
the afternoon iridesces.

Its basalt tones fully
besiege the ocean water
—peaceful aquamarine.

The flow of consciousness
iridesces:
blue-gray,
afternoon in flight,
a snare for the night
with its daring telescope.

Don Carlos, which is
           the blue-green star
                    of memory?

(English translation by David Bowles)

¡Soy Quetzal!

Arraigada
a tu cielo
no conozco
de fronteras

Mi plumaje
elegante
roza llanos
que me claman

Es tu brisa
que me guía
a senderos
que no anclan

¡Soy Quetzal!

Tengo alas
con matices
rojo vivo
verde fluido.

Soberanamente,

yo navego
en tu cielo
donde todos

Nos cruzamos,
Nos miramos—

Con mi pecho
bien erguido

Rooted to
Your sky
I know no
Borders

My elegant
Feathers
Graze meadows
Which claim
My name

It is your breeze
That guides me
Toward land

That does not
Anchor me

¡Soy Quetzal!

My wings
Have tones of
Vibrant reds
Fluid greens.

Sovereignly,

I navigate
Your skies
Where we all

Cross, gaze
And harmonize—

impregno el viento

Que me hechiza
a encarnar
la libertad.

With my
Expanded chest
I impregnate
The wind

Enticing me
To embody
Liberty.

Claudia D. Hernández

(English translation by José Hernández Díaz)

hembras

ríen / lloran / rezongan

no callan
y cuando hablan
no mienten

de vez en cuando
se muerden la
lengua

escupen,
no se tragan
su propia sangre

sus sátiras
renacen en medio
de realidades

con disimulo
encarnan el
cinismo

desafían,

deslumbran
al estallar en nuestra
presencia

viven / mueren / inspiran

They laugh/ they cry/
they howl

They are never silent
And when they speak
They do not lie

Now and then,
They bite their
Tongues

They expel,
They do not swallow
Their own blood

Their satires are
Reborn amidst
Realities

Cunningly,
They incarnate
Cynicism

They defy,

When they fade
They explode
Into supernovas
Blinding us

They live/
They die/
They inspire

All of us.

Claudia D. Hernández

(English translation by José Hernández Díaz)

Rompiendo el silencio

(para nuestras hermanas en Juárez)

Mientras el sol
penetra cada nube,

se esclarece el cielo,

revelando
su cadáver
descompuesto—

Desnuda,
ha sido abandonada
en pleno desierto:

—no se encuentra
        no regresa—

Su alma entera
ha sido mutilada.

Se la llevan viva;
La regresan muerta.

Atormentados,
todos rezan:

—no se encuentra
        no regresa—

Shattered Silence

(for our sisters in Juárez)

As the sun
Pierces the clouds,

The sky clears,

Revealing her
Decomposing corpse—

Naked,
She has been abandoned
In the desert plain:

—She cannot be found
  She has not returned—

Her soul
Has been mutilated.

They took her whole;
They return her dead.

Tormented,
Her family prays:

—She cannot be found
She has not returned—

Todos lloran,

Elevando sus miradas
a ese cielo despejado—

Torturados,
se dan cuenta
que nadie escucha...

Claudia D. Hernández

Everyone cries,

Elevating their eyes
To the clear sky—

Tortured,
They notice that
No one listens…

(English translation by José Hernández Díaz)

Las dos lenguas

Mi idioma es una pared pintada
de obsesiones blancas y negras,
es una pared alzada en un desierto,
aquí también hace mucho frío por las noches,
por el día se detienen a descansar
algunos tristes pájaros.
Mi idioma es una pared
alzada sin fin,
cuya sombra cae sobre mi sombra.
Es una pared de huesos,
con coyunturas profundas
 por donde pueden verse las extensiones
de mi realidad, buscando verte desarmado.
Pero no ves tú ni la pared,
ni los huesos, ni el desierto,
ajenos a ti son los pájaros tristes,
mismos que son origen de mi idioma.
Para ti no existe nada más que tu lengua,
esa criatura fría
que se adueña de todo territorio.
Una lengua agria que no conoce otro comienzo
que su propia descendencia.
Para ti sólo existe tu lengua viperina,
lengua de serpiente que ha buscado
acorralarme desde el día que llegó a mi tierra
y comenzó a construir sobre mí
ésta pared que me ahoga.
Tu lengua es la serpiente
que busca por las calles,
en las leyes y en las escuelas,
encontrar mi lengua
para cercenarla,
para arrancar de tajo

The Two Tongues

My language is a wall painted
with black and white obsessions,
a wall erected in the desert—
it's also cold here most nights
and during the day a few hapless birds
stop to rest.
My language is a wall
that is endlessly erected,
whose shadow falls across my shadow.
It's a wall of bones,
of deep joints
along which the extensions of my reality
can be glimpsed, hoping to see you dismantled.
But you don't see the wall,
the bones, or the desert—
foreign to you are the hapless birds,
those that give rise to my language.
For you nothing exists but your tongue,
that cold creature
that seizes every territory.
A bitter tongue that knows no other beginning
than its own ancestry.
For you only your venomous tongue exists,
that serpent tongue that has sought
to corral me since it arrived in my land
and began to build on my very back
that wall that now suffocates me.
Your tongue is the snake
that scours the streets,
the laws, the schools,
hunting for my tongue
to sever it,
to rip out at the root

el único pedazo de mí
que germina con el dulce canto
de mi madre.
Busca serpentina, mi lengua errante,
mi lengua de necesidades básicas,
mi lengua sumisa que simplemente busca
una humilde tregua por las tardes,
esas tardes que tu lengua siente
que también son suyas.
Buscas mi lengua
para arrancarla, para colocarla
junto a todas las otras lenguas que has arrancado.
Mis hermanos ya no entienden mis canciones,
no reconocen mi mano
que sujetó su mano por siglos enteros,
y no puedo gritarles
porque mostraría mi lengua desnuda
y vulnerable, y seguirías su olor
de flores y tierra fresca.
Mi idioma es una pared
con la que has impuesto tu idioma,
cada piedra la colocaste con saña.
Nuestras lenguas luchan
en una superficie no visible.
Mi lengua es la vida
que siembra cuidadosa por túneles secretos.
Tu lengua me persigue carnívora,
mi lengua sobrevive.
Mi lengua es la vida
arrullando a hijos y hermanos.
Mi lengua es la vida
agua limpia que busca redimir tu opresión.
Mi lengua es la vida
hay un mar de paz
al otro lado de esta pared.

the only piece of me
in which the sweet song
of my mother sprouts.
Serpentine it hunts my wandering tongue,
my tongue of basic necessities,
my submissive tongue that only seeks
a humble truce in the afternoons,
those afternoons your tongue believes
are also yours.
You seek my tongue
to tear it out, to place it
next to all the other tongues you've torn out.
My brothers no longer understand my songs,
they don't recognize my hand
that held their hands for entire centuries,
and I cannot cry out to them
because that would display my naked
and vulnerable tongue, and you would track its scent
of flowers and fresh earth.
My language is a wall
with which you have imposed your language,
every stone laid with viciousness.
Our tongues struggle
upon an invisible surface.
My tongue is life,
seeded cautiously through secret tunnels.
Your tongue pursues me, carnivorous;
my tongue survives.
My tongue is life,
crooning to children and siblings.
My tongue is life,
clean water that seeks to redeem your oppression.
My tongue is life—
there is an ocean of peace
on the other side of this wall.

No tengas miedo.
Mi lengua es la vida.

Rossy Evelin Lima

Don't be afraid.
My tongue is life.

(English translation by David Bowles)

Indio barro

Niqitoa ni Nesaualkoyotl:
Esperanza, sol, barro.
Se marcha, con el sol a cuestas,
esperanza, barro en las piernas
en el corazón barro,
¿Kuix ok neli nemoua in tlaltikpak?
Entre agujeros se acuesta.
En el penar lleva su cruz,
cruz impuesta, cruz y barro.
An nochipa tlaltikpak:
Les habla a sus dioses,
los mira entre sueños,
los toca con ansia,
con ansia, entre hierbas.
Se quita la ropa, temazcal,
y talla su esencia de indio y barro.
San achika ya nikan.
El indio se cansa,
su cabeza gacha, su espalda encorvada,
al amo sirve, al dios alaba,
en el temazcal se desviste.
Ahí está su figura, su figura y barro.
Tel ka chalchiuitl no xamani.
No quiere, pero lo sigue viendo,
se despoja de cadenas,
cicatrices,
se arranca su lengua,
sigue a sus dioses hablando.
No teokuitlatl in tlapani.
Aquí adentro, aúlla y se hunde,
con sus hierbas se azota,
se tira y se hunde.

Clay Indian

Niqitoa ni Nesaualkoyotl:
Hope, sun, clay.
He departs, the sun on his back,
hope, clay on his legs,
in his heart clay,
Kuix ok neli nemoua in tlaltikpak?
Amidst holes he lies down.
In his suffering he bears his cross,
a cross imposed, cross and clay.
An nochipa tlaltikpak:
He speaks to his gods,
he sees them in dreams,
he touches them anxiously,
anxiously, amidst the herbs.
He takes off his clothes, *temazcal* sweat lodge,
and scrubs at his essence of Indian and clay.
San achika ya nikan.
The Indian grows tired,
his head low, his spine bent,
serving the master, praising the Lord,
in the *temazcal* he removes his clothes.
There is his shape, his shape and clay.
Tel ka chalchiuitl no xamani.
Unwilling, he keeps watching it,
stripping off chains,
scars—
he rips out his tongue
but continues to speak to his gods.
No teokuitlatl in tlapani.
Here inside he howls and sinks,
flagellates himself with herbs,
throws himself down and sinks.

No ketsali posteki.
Respira con fuerza,
endereza la espalda,
no se le borra al indio
la mirada agachada,
se endereza y se siente
volador, pájaro,
que muere por ser moreno,
moreno, barro.
Y piensa el indio,
soy barro, mi espalda
la amolda la voluntad de mi amo
An nochipa tlaltikpak:
El indio no grita,
el pecho se le pudre
por no estar gritando,
se muerde la boca
y exige y tiembla,
cuando habla en su lengua
se siente capaz.
En la oscuridad se retuerce,
indio sol, indio barro
san achika ye nikan.
Llora sobre tu piedra,
arráncate con las manos el llanto,
pero vuelve
indio barro,
esperanza, barro.

Rossy Evelin Lima

No ketsali posteki.
He breathes heavily,
straightens his back,
but the Indian's downcast
eyes do not lift.
He straightens and feels
he flies, bird-like,
dying because he is brown,
dark, clay.
And the Indian thinks,
I am clay, my back
molded by my master's will.
An nochipa tlaltikpak:
The Indian does not scream:
his breast rots away
for want of screaming;
he bites his tongue
and demands and trembles—
when he speaks in his language
he feels adept.
In the darkness he squirms,
sun Indian, clay Indian,
san achika ye nikan.
Cry over your stone,
with your very hands drag sobs from within,
but remain
clay Indian,
hope, clay.

(English translation by David Bowles)

My City

We are two drops of water,
you are my city.
I left you years ago,
untouched by the hunger of a better future,
I took your rocks to build a new road
and the leaves of your banana trees
to make a hood for my dreams.
I traveled away; many times I looked back at you
and saw myself waving good bye.
I walked slowly,
climbing through the walls of a new country,
I hid from the new trees, new air, new spaces,
I could not recognize my face in any mirror,
you were not there.
We are two drops of water.
You started changing,
while my steps were melting my feet,
dragging away from you.
You didn't say anything when they took
the *framboyanes* from your soil.
I did, I said no, and my mouth was shut,
I did, and refused to swallow the new language,
I did, and my eyes looked down desperate to find
the smell of your blue waves.
I was the outsider, still gardening your memory
but I was running out of rocks.
I wanted to go back to you,
we are two drops of water,
I needed to see your face, my face
I couldn't find you,
the flow of a new river
is now running through my eyes.
The last rock of my winding road

is the memory of you
skipping across your quite waters.
You will always be my city,
by the roots sprouting in my heart.
Today, my dreams are no longer hidden
I am a drop of water.

Rossy Evelin Lima

Canto azul

No one has seen us. We have seen
no one, blind as we are from seeing.
-Miguel Hernández.

Capitalism is exploitation
is human trafficking   is
        maquiladoras are
feminicides are   bloody
  rivers are   Cuidad Juárez
    is not for sale.   If we
speak if   we write   if
we act   if we fight   if
we   i   m   a   g   i   n   e
if we unite: Cuidad Juárez
            Will not be sold.

Nadie nos ha visto. Hemos visto
a nadie, ciegos como estamos de ver.
-Miguel Hernández.

El capitalismo es la explotación
es   el trafico humano   es
        las maquiladoras son
los feminicidios   son   los ríos
sangrantes son   Ciudad Juárez
          no está de venta.   Si
hablamos   si escribimos   si
actuamos   si luchamos   si
lo   i   m   á   g   i   n   a   m   o   s
si nos unimos: Ciudad Juárez
            No será vendida.

José Hernández Díaz

Juárez en llamas

HAY cementerios solos,
tumbas llenas de huesos sin sonido,
el corazón pasando un túnel
oscuro, oscuro, oscuro...

—*Pablo Neruda,* Sólo la Muerte.

In Ciudad Juárez,

our sisters
perish from the
influence of
the Yankee dollar
on the machete:

there is thunder
in the sky—

we are nothing
if we hide.

In Ciudad Juárez,

our daughters
weaken in the
maquiladoras
of the tyrant:

they will never
know the sun—

we are nothing
if we run.

In Ciudad Juárez,

our mothers
mourn in the
Cathedral de
Guadalupe:

their tired tears
turn to rivers—

we are nothing
if we're silent.

José Hernández Díaz

Nopales for Breakfast

maybe one day
they'll finally use
that key they carry
forever in their pocket

—Francisco X. Alarcón, Poor Poets.

My *abuela* is
Preparing the
Nopales
In the kitchen--
It is dawn.

As she cuts
Away at the
Flesh of
The ancient
Plant,
Stripping it
Of its thorns,
I see
Our future,
Raza:

It is just
As green;
It is fertile
And tangible.

We are those
Tranquil *campos*
Where the
Verduras

Originate and flourish;
We have discovered
Boundless oceans
In our
Humble gardens.

The memory
Of the last
Harvest still
Resides
On our
Sweaty palms.

We are those
Seeds of
Love and honor--
The same ones
Implanted in us
By our
Proud ancestors.

Will you wash
Away at
Your strong,
Brown palms,
Raza?

Will you try
And cleanse
Your flesh of
That memory?

Will you flee
To the
Concrete city
At sunset?

Hungry for
Profits;

Hungry for
Television;

Hungry for
Clothing;

Starving for
Assimilation?

Do your
Knuckles
Not bleed:

*Azteca
Turquoise?*

*P'urhépecha
Bronze?*

*Zapotec
Indigo?*

Try and
Punch the
Spray-painted
Gutters
In your *barrio*,
Raza,
And tell me
What color
Your knuckles
Bleed.

Tell me,
Raza.

José Hernández Díaz

Dying

Damn you
For dying all alone in your apartment
For dying slowly in a place I will never see
For dying in my arms when I had barely met you
And for all this dying
You will never watch Food Network with me again
You will never show me how everything I think I know about
you is wrong
You will never come to my bed at night so that I can slay your
nightmares
I am left knowing
There was nothing I could do
There was nothing I could do
And there is nothing I can do now
Except love you till the very last breath
And beyond, until the end of mine
All I can do is love someone
The way I should have loved you
So that you would not believe the only way out
Was your dying
So that you will know that all those years
I loved you still
So that you would know that I will never love another
Like I loved you
All I can do is damn your dying
Whether slowly or all at once
I will use every tear
To weather your name into the stone that is my heart
Etch it to the depth of the Grand Canyon
A hole that nothing can ever fill
A crevice that I created with the love I had
The love I have
The love I have left over

Choking on it
As I say goodbye
Slowly, or all at once
Damn your dying.

Vanessa Brown

To the Young Lady

At the McDonald's Drive-thru Window (La Joya)

First, let me begin with an apology
I'm sorry I ordered two sausage and egg biscuits,
hold the biscuit
also, I'm quite impressed that your computer has a
NO BISQ button
when I pull up the first window, I imagine the person who fits
the garbled, distorted voice in the box who took my order
who punched in
2 SSG/EGG
NO BISQ
COF
2 SPL
2 CRM
PREP
I try to imagine what a person that garbled would look like
but you appear quite normal
and concerned when I hand you three dollars
and begin counting out the additional $1.67 in change
instead of the expected 5 dollar bill
you adjusted though, when you noticed I gave you
two cents more
so you could give me back a nickel
and I could get rid of two pennies
just so you know, I also rubbed those in
antibacterial hand sanitizer
you don't know the kinds of germs that are on change
it's pretty gross
Our transaction ends with
a nickel, a receipt and a command
pull up to the next window
except that now we're stuck in drive thru limbo

because there are two cars in front of me
and i don't know whether to engage you in
stimulating conversation about the Republican Primaries
or roll up my window and pretend you are not there
I tense and I assume that the decision is mine
do I act like a snob and ignore you
pretend you are suddenly invisible
in your visor, name badge and uniform shirt
should I ask what kind of shoes you have on
or what your goals are within the larger
McDonalds Organization
you, trained professional that you are
smile at my internal struggle
notice my hand tensed above the window button
have already moved on to the next caffeine starved person
and liberated me
from the bonds of limbo

Vanessa Brown

On Human Evolution

When future archeologists dig up my bones
And brush the dirt of eons
Off my remains
Will they call me *homo habilus*?
Because of my large brain
Full of useless knowledge –
Passwords, memories and recipes
And patterns of ancestors before me.
Will they call me *homo erectus*?
Because I've learned to stand tall,
Stand up for myself, for us,
Off my paws and on my own feet.
Will they call me *Australopithecus*?
Because I drag my feet
The way they dragged their knuckles,
Slowing myself down
Leaving tracks behind me
Not wanting to go on, not able to stop.
Will they give me a new name?
Homo mommy?
Woman erectus?
Stooped shoulders from daily burdens,
Wide hips for birthing civilization.
Or will they cast my bones aside –
Useless frame to fragile body,
And give me no name?
Because they cannot excavate my heart,
That beat
From Australopithecus
To erectus,
Friend to lover,
Habilus to sapien,
Woman to mother.

Nothing,
To everything,
To nothing.

Vanessa Brown

Thank God I Divorced

My "TED" before I Stuck My Head in an Oven

I am convinced
I busted our dynamo a few years ago
and became a slave to the North Sea

the final accounts of our historic events
make me feel full
like watching too much television
and eating too many sweets
like filling my belly with processed foods
that only make me fatter

and so I linger in space
still looking for the mother ship
still searching for a heart
one that beats with the oceans tide
I still wonder why you shaved your beard
and cut your hair
why you stopped looking for aliens
through your Wal- Mart telescope
on bitter autumn nights

sharing a bed with a stranger is like
looking at an abstract painting through the eyes of
a politician
one without an ounce of intellect
who calls creativity a sin

it suffocates me
and satisfies me
kills my soul
but gives me pleasure
expires my philosophy

If being a writer has a formula
I still have not learned it
I still stain my lips with ink
I still dissolve sentences in the dark
I still call the moon my lover
I still dance on thin ice
I still let the dust pile up
I have grown found of this isolation

Because I have so many days to fill
journals to saturate
verses to edit
stories to summon
jaded characters to conjure

and so the days pass
months eat years
years birth peace
drunk on ten dollar wine
spilling bouts of introspect
sometimes I remember to pray
but forget phrases
photographs
and scenes
it's all backwards
and some days its forward

some days the moon refuses to close its eyes
other days the sun does not set
some days its peace
and other days it is warfare
fought in the trenches
some days its Ted and Sylvia
Frida and Diego
other days are a feminist evolution
one that annihilates the males species
the year 2012 is mostly filled with prospects
and uncertainties
with poems
and longing
with love
and the absence of love
with songs that can not be silenced
songs that refuse to be silenced

if days are dismal
I intend to bleach them
Because I would NEVER EVER EVER go back
Thank God I divorced my "TED"
before I stuck my head in an oven

Rachel Vela

Postcard from New York City

Arrived at La Guardia
7 PM
Heard all the bells whistles
And clamor
Instantly fell in love

Got lost on the streets of Harlem
Heard a gun shot three blocks away
Bought a knock off Louis Vuitton wallet
In China Town
Ate too many carbs in Little Italy
Flirted with the waiter

Walked the Brooklyn Bridge
The sun pleasantly wrapped
Itself around me

Twilight stroll
In Soho
Dinner in Manhattan
Drinks in Willamsburg
Hipsters as far as the eye can see
Witch House
And Indie Music blasting around every street corner
Took the wrong train back
Made love to a stranger on the train
New York invited me to stay
To stay warm by its undying fire

As of now
No plans to return to the desert

Rachel Vela

Colorado Street 78570

On Colorado Street
my grandfather Jose still fixes cars
and lets illegal aliens work on cars in his garage
my grandmother Senida still fills summer mornings with the smell of
Folgers coffee and beans cooking on the gas stove
my brother still plays outside late at night
he and the other neighborhood kids
still listen for the sinister whistle of the lechusa

On Colorado Street
the smell of rain still blows through open windows
I still lay in my bed listening to punk music
while reading Jane Austin
I'm still 15 years old

On Colorado Street
my hair is pink
 The Sex Pistols
blast out vulgarities
offending my Christian family
my grandmother tries to teach me to knit and sew
I fight with my brother because he's smoking weed in the alley
with the neighbors
I am 17 years old and 8 months pregnant
On Colorado Street I marry the man I'm suppose to love till
death do us part
with doubt and fear I become his wife
I become a mother
12 years later I lay on my grandmother's bed
grieving
detached from my former life
and recall the doubt that consumed me the day I said "I do"

On Colorado Street
my family gathers after we bury my grandfather
I smell his clothes
I gather his books and his bibke
I watch my uncle mourn for his dad
his best friend
I listen to my aunts sing Spanish hymns
"*Un día a la vez*"

ON Colorado Street
the house changes
the earth shifts
summer nights become shorter
the stars lose their mystical twinkle
the lechusas no longer whistle
my grandmothers rose bushes die
the grass withers
along with spring afternoons
nothing smells the same
everything is cement
and paved
and I am 33 years old...

Rachel Vela

Lullabye for the Immigrant Ocelot

O mother cat, come race again by my side

your abandoned kitten anticipates
the continuance of your truncated
lessons slashed short by the blade of a wall
standing like a cleaver stuck in dead meat

I lie in wait for you   here
in the river brush shade

my dignified companions parted from
kin divided like seas at Moses' feet
the jaguarundi and the roadrunner
the chachalaca and the antelope

they keep me company   here
by the guillotine fence

until you are ready to cross over
then, I will rest my head once more upon
your spotted back and coil in your warmth
our slick mounds rising and falling in unison

when we slumber again   here
in the river brush shade

for we all drift into sleep curled up tight
then, when dreams unfurl we fan out like fists
unclasped or flags stretched on the horizon
y me arrullaras hasta que me duerme.

Amalia Ortiz

Amor Peligroso

¡Wátchale!

You, with that Big Red in your brown hand!
El doctor dice que será mi muerte.
Bad for my *alta presión* y the cause
of my diabetes con *su* caffeine
y corn syrup. *¡Te pone bien loco!*
Ten cuidado y think before you drink!

Pues, it's too late for me. Since the young age
of three, *mi mami* had me hooked licking
sticky *líquido* by the *lengua*ful
de mi tetera—red coating my tongue.
I had no idea the sweat treat in
my tummy would someday cost me my teeth.

¡De versa! ¡Soy adicta! Now my heart
pumps saccharine sangre. And I'm told if I
don't say *adios,* it could cost me my toes
like my Tía Toñya whose sweet tooth took
her big toes in exchange for a lifetime
of munching Butterfinger *y* Baby Ruth.

This is more than addiction. This is love—
in all its self-destruction. *¡Peligroso!*
¡Amor podoroso! Si fuera posible,
I'd say the drink gave me *ojo*—with that
mysterious taste, hard to define taste...
like liquid bubble gum, or like pop-rocks,

like *nada natural… Pues*, it tastes red.
redder than the fruit of the prickly pear
redder than juice of the Ruby Red
red like *el diablo* who made and cursed it.
Te embruja, and will not release you
from its spell until it takes your toes!

¡Wátchale!

Amalia Ortiz

These Hands

Which Have Never Picked Cotton

My father unexpectedly pulled the car to the side
of the interstate and ordered his four children out
into the cotton field. Confused, we set down our
video games, flipped off the headphones,
and reluctantly followed.

He said, "You've never picked cotton.
You have no idea what it's like.
It looks so soft, but it has thorns
which cut at the fingers and draw
blood even through gloves.

We mortified teens reached down with sideways
glances embarrassed by the passing cars. We
plucked tiny clouds while rolling eyes and
swallowed a hand full of humble. But the real lesson
would not be digested until years later.

They say the first generation sacrifices,
so that the second generation can achieve,
only for the third generation to squander.
And these third generation hands–
These hands have never picked cotton.

These hands which have never picked cotton—
more overindulged than industrious —
as tender as Abuelo's whispers—

These hands have never felt the prick of burrs
scrape deep or puncture flesh.

These fruitless hands which have never plucked grapes
from the vine are strangers to orange groves and grapefruit
rows. These fragile knuckles have never scraped over
washboards or scrubbed floors for money, but
have been caressed by Abuela who did so in my place.

These hands, which have spent more hours pushing buttons
than planting with these fingertips—
uncalloused as the fulfillment of grandmother's wishes–
tender as this back which has never ached in labor–
never felt the sun baked flesh stretched beyond endurance–

This body may not know, but must never forget.
These hands which have never worked leather
hammered heels, yanked soles, repaired saddles
sanded and polished shoes—
Grandpa did, so that I may not.

They say the first generation sacrifices,
the second generation achieves,
for the third generation to squander.
And these third generation hands need to find
purpose. These empty hands hold so much promise.

These hands which have never picked cotton—
This body—
the bones, muscle, youth not yet sacrificed to feed children—
This body understands struggle builds character,
but is still searching for what these hands will build.

These selfish hands—these lazy, delicate hands—
assimilated American made–
These idle devil's playthings play
dead as if incapable of growing, crafting, sculpting
a new American with these hands —

These hands which have never loaded weapons—
These eyes which have never stared war in the face
sparred by Dad's tour of duty claim all these things
I've never done. The softness of this body feels Dad's
scars etched someplace on the skin of my soul.

These legs which have never hiked foreign jungles—
Are these legs so untested that they will be the first generation
not able to support their own weight? Will they buckle
only to lie around and lounge? Was that Abuelo's goal
moving to this land of 3rd, 4th, 5th generations,

where what comes easily goes unesteemed as these hands
cover the ignorantly bored yawn of privilege?
These hands which have never picked cotton
become more American at rest—softer, dumber—
Their long-term memory loss bashes that next

generation of immigrants who dare aspire to my luxury
of laziness resting on these feet which have never walked
factory floors—spent more time marching in protest than
harvesting produce— These clumsy hands—
more hours in libraries than in labor—in classrooms than

cleaning public bathrooms—more toys than tools—
more theory than action—These grateful hands write
words of hope—of remembering and being remembered—
give back this gift—scratch feeble offerings
to those who came before these hands—

These reverent hands grapple to fold together the past
and the present like hands folding in prayer
in the tradition of my Abuela, Visabuela, Tatabuela—
pray to their same god my modern concerns—
to remember and be remembered

These feet stand on shoulders
reaching down not to pick cotton
but to pull up the next generation.
These words are for you—
to remember and be remembered.

These hands which have never picked cotton are ready
to park the car at the side of the road, snap
the children out of their stupor, and order them
into the fields to appreciate the art of craft—
of digging in the earth as creators.

If struggle breeds character
and sloth a deadly sin,
then I am either the harvest
my ancestors cultivated,
or their sacrifices sinfully squandered.

They say the first generation sacrifices,
the second achieves,
for the third to squander, and these
third generation hands which have never picked cotton–
These obligated hands are not my own.

Amalia Ortiz

That Shadowy Thing

There's a black figure in front of me
It moves the same way as I do and has my shape.
The figure is like me because it is me.
Darkness is my reflection, my true form—
Always been that way.

That's what I am.

I'm neither Venus nor Adonis,
My face has no features to attract the sexes,
Nor do I have a voice to lure them into my arms.
I am only a void with nothing to prove,
Having no rights to give or receive.

Not he or she.

Where is the ring to slip onto a lover's index?
Where is the key to unlock the sacred chest?
Where is Medusa's head to petrify the men?
Where is the sword to slay the kidnapping dragon?
Where have they been hiding all this time?

Nothing below.

I have none of those things to be admired.
A thing that lacks only arouses fear and paranoia,
It never brings ecstasy and affection.
A black sheet which can't be drawn or colored on.
A living silhouette is what I am.

A shadowy thing.

Diana Elizondo

The Circus

Tonight is the circus's final night
And the spectacles are filled with atrocities and odd charades.
Things that make people frown, but are still entertaining,
They keep telling themselves it's just a show, not actual events.
The fire starters, the psycho gunners
and the well groomed chimps
exit the stage leaving ashes, blood and feces in the spotlight.

The oblivious clowns bow
after performing their lackluster stunts.
The audience laughs at the overdosed jesters
as they stumble out the ring
with man-made smiles stretching
across their smeared painted faces.

But the crowd has already seen it all
and they are tired of the endless encores.
They saw every gruesome act performed
by the troubled performers
and the senseless tricks from the lethargic harlequins.
The ringmaster in the patched-up top hat realizes
the exploitation has to end.
The tent is going down and the show is finally done.
The freaks are gone and so are the clowns.

The circus is now reduced to a barren field
littered with posters of unruly divas and stars.

Diana Elizondo

Irony

Free kittens.
Saying "I'll never."
It doesn't matter what it looks like,
I'll drive it.

A Chevette with a green door?
Red hood, blue roof, and
A yellow bumper?
You'll drive it?

Saying good-bye to the man you love,
Breaking your own heart,
Because you know
You deserve so much better.

I have a cat- she wasn't free.
I no longer say "I'll never."
I have a car all the same color.

A Honda Accord with a black door,
Black hood, black roof, and
A black bumper.

Saying hello to the man you still love,
Letting him put your heart back together,
Because you know
No one else will love you better.

Kristin Keith

Faith

*(For my Great Grandmother,
A woman I only know from pictures.)*

As I look at your picture,
The one on the wall,
I see the corners of your mouth
Turned up, ever so slightly.

I wonder,
Mona Lisa,
Why don't you smile?

Was it when you lost Hope?
Did your smile die with her?

Was it the Great Depression?
Did your smile collapse with the stock market?

Was it because
In the midst of the joy of your daughter's birth,
It disappeared with your dream of children not to be?

As I look at your picture,
The one on my wall,
I see the corners of your mouth
Turned up, ever so slightly.

I wonder,
Faith,
Why don't you smile?

Kristin Keith

So Much More

It's hard to think the man,
Riding beside me,
Isn't what he used to be.

He looks the same.
He acts the same.
He sounds the same.

But now—
There is a slight stumble in his step.
A tiring in his eyes,
I've never seen before.

He lets me drive more.
He has to stop for the night,
When we used to drive straight through.

He looks the same.
He acts the same.
He sounds the same.

But now—
He's frustrated.
He doesn't think like before.

He looks the same.
He acts the same.
He sound the same.

But now—
He carries a cane,
110 years old, it carried my grandfather
Before.

He looks the same.
He acts the same.
He sounds the same.

The Stroke—
It could have taken
So. Much. More.

Kristin Keith

Negra

Amnesia, that's what I call it.
Completely forgot where I was going.
I hang around with my own desires
Without worrying about time.
Everything could wait, but not love...
Later, I learned true love waits for me.
Made mistakes, yes: sorry for the delay.
I'm not finished; as a matter of fact, I don't think I will ever be.
I need lessons once in a while to learn what I learned today—
To wait...

Arleen

you know...
I've always wondered if there was a time when you really loved me...
don't worry I'll stop...
I'll leave you alone: just hang in there for a little bit more...
let me cry out all these feelings.
Let me tell you how much you meant to me...
you were everything I wanted for me...
I was happy with you.

I don't ask God *what about me?*
I trust his time,
his love and whatever He has for me.
I had the right to conquer you
and run after you
if that was my choice...
but I waited and waited on Him...
and at the end... He said no...
why? Don't know or want to know now.
I trust his plan, so bye.

María Piedra

Us

The old wooden door opens
a sideways mouth with no teeth
smoke and music drool from it as they step in
there
at the corner bar
the one with three letters and no name
where men in dresses and cowboys meet
while Selena and Madonna sing
there
where the music and makeup is loud
where the drinks are strong and cheap
they can hold hands
they can embrace
they can finally be

deep in the darkest corner
where the floor is sticky with yesterday's booze
where the light is yellow and dim
where the grimy mirror is cracked into three
there
they can finally kiss
no one stares
no one sneers
no one calls out hateful names
there
drowning in each other's lips
all falls into oblivion
there is no music, no smoke, no sticky floors
no fear of the *machista*'s fists outside
no condemning Bible bullies spitting hell
nothing matters only them

Outside
drifting along the murky Rio Grande
among the swaying palms and mesquite trees
the sightless world sleeps and dreams
baptized in sticky South Texas sweat
they cling feverishly to dusty secrets and musty roots
there
lulled by the rhythmic hymns
of hand-me-down hate and ignorance
all falls into oblivion
and nothing matters only them.

César de León

Let It Rain

Open the window
let me hear
the drumming and dripping
of the sacred rain
      against the cloudy glass
while blue smoke
sticks to my hands
      ashes folding quietly
      beneath my fingernails

Let me hear
the murmuring wind
recount the legends of the Rio Grande
      where the children of the sun
      no longer play
      among the giant carrizos
let it speak
      of cotton fields
      in August
      sweaty blistered hands
dancing devils and weeping women
      syrupy Valley nights
      sugar cane dreams
golden   unpaved streets

Open the door
let the smell of wet dirt
swallow me
let my feet absorb
the baptismal waters
      through silver gray callouses
      through bare and brittle caliche bones
      through thorn scraped knees

Let me hear
      the tired praying multitudes in every drop
      dripping   slipping   drowning
      sopping milk with
      dusty   ragged   dollars
in barbed wire snagged shirts
over plastic rosaries

Open every window!
Open every door!
Open the sky!
Open the temples of Tlaloc!
Open the past!
Open the future!
Open the God-damned world!
      and let it rain!

César de León

Frontera Dust

There is dirt on our faces
      gray dirt
it blows across the river
      back and forth
from Monterrey to Hidalgo
      back and forth
from Reynosa to Brownsville
gritty and dusty
      it covers our skin
      crusts our eyes
      tickles our nose
up along the carretera it gusts
flying down expressway 83

Can you see it?
dry and gray with speckles of red
      can you taste it?
can you taste
the tiny motes of blood
that pepper it?
Yes?
      No?

It pools along the road
      anonymous
      invisible
in marbled puddles of red and gray
slowly drying
      bloody dirt
         dirty blood
      naked dust
left behind by the thirsty sun
      it hides

in the rusty wind
in the skeletal moonlight
a deep dark whirl
      enormous
blacker than the night
      obsidian fear
        no   one   sees
gray amnesia
        no one knows
voiceless it crosses the river
      back and forth
back   and   forth

César de León

Storyteller

When the night approaches
there is no one left, but
you and I,
River.

You know all the stories
of men and women
crossing their children
into the heat of Texas.
When your water rises
emotions wave
and history, begins at your riverbank.
You echo their cries
and desperation, River.
You sing me their songs
every night
as the wolves howl
that they are present.
They fight your purpose
and pilgrimage across
over the manmade walls.
You are not their enemy
but you are not
their friend either.

You are a messenger,
the old storyteller.

Clarrissia Nerio

Camino

Every morning, on the way to work
I drive by the fields
and I see them
rows and rows of grapefruits
oranges
tomatoes
onions
hidden under long sleeved shirts
and sombreros.
They are migrant workers.
Backs up to the unmerciful sun
knees on the ground
like when in prayer.
With their heads down, sweat
runs down their backbone
and dirt blinks off their lashes.
I see their baskets
colorful and yet
heavy, like the culture.
I keep going. Drive past them.
Their weary faces stay on my mind
and grow like the seeds
that are dug deep into Valley dirt.
The soil they touch
with the skin on their hands so hard
they break and bleed
hold the trails
of their brothers
sisters
aunts
and cousins.
They walk in a line

The same line their children won't walk
because they are on their way to work.

Clarrissia Nerio

Surrender

This feeling is unexpected, it's so strange.
Intense emotions shaking my troubled soul.
Shame, nostalgia, anger, love.
An immense sadness concluding a cycle of nothing.
It is not for certain, but I think
this is the end.

The internal war and mischief have come to an end.
Surviving on my own shouldn't be this strange.
I need to learn to let go, but I think
only God can save my treacherous soul
No matter what I do, nothing
has been able to complete me, but His Love.

I recall the pursuit for an unconditional love
Looking high and low without end.
Searching, seeking in all the wrong places finding nothing.
Hopelessness seeping in like a strange
Smooth liquid, burning every scrap of my soul.
I couldn't feel. I couldn't think.

What was I thinking?
What was I to do without his love?
All these doubts incessantly stabbing at my soul.
Dark melancholy indicating the end.
Unable to forgive and forget in this cruel and strange
world, I crept towards salvation. It was better
          than doing nothing.

Yet He had asked for nothing.
And somehow peace and forgiveness found me, to think,
It was in this desolate, solitary confinement. Strange,
No longer holding on to the deceitful love.

Finally discovering the thread that will end
The gorging of my decaying soul.

Only You can save my soul.
I had to lose everything to know there is nothing
else that would have been able to end
this immeasurable sorrow and pain. I think
giving up and letting go were the only ways to find Your Love.
"*Joy would come in the morning*," no longer feels so strange.

At the end of it all, my soul learned to hope.
Strange as it may seem, there was nothing left
        to say after the goodbyes.
    And to think that all I had to do was just accept His Love.

Yolanda López

Be Still

The sky is tinted
Shades of purple, white and gold.
And the earth stands still...

Lullaby

The mockingbird sings
Every night beyond the gates—
Tender lullaby.

.

Yolanda López

Finding Home

She was a quiet, brown-skinned little girl
pushed away from the comforts of her memories and
her second-story home. She tried to find out where she belonged
as she laid her tear-stricken face down on a pink pillow
             on the hardwood floor.
Remembering her childhood friends, forced to grow up
beyond her years, while she got lost in a foreign language
             and puddles of fears.
Finding refuge in the thunderous symphony
             of a sorrowful trombone;
Solemnly walking home, carrying dreams and hiding
             in stories of fantasy.
Until one day she was startled by the realization her
limbs were growing roots in that strange land.
Discovering new passions prowling inside her unraveling mind;
"*This American dream will be mine*," she confessed
             to the winds.
Nothing would hinder her desire to succeed.
No more broken promises. No more black and blue vellum.
She found her peace wrapped around Jeremiah
             twenty-nine, eleven.
Her soul will forever rest serenely along Mexican plains.
Her heart will eternally glimmer red, white and blue.
Violeta found her home at last.

Yolanda López

Balacera en Reynosa

gunshots echo as a man lies dead, a border street
in downtown Reynosa where sun setting clouds
are heavy with repeated mourning and rival
emotions flare

guards on the balconied stairways outside
darkened warehouses watch each other drag and
cuff who protest, fallen by blasts'

heat, humidity steep as a widow kneels by her
husband's newly-dead body, crying out anger in
a scene not unlike any other when accordions
and guitars play

corridos of the wars in ode to prominent trades,
and the crowd grows and gathers amid the fast
beat of the music because that's what they heard
first from a distance

masked guards continue their revolt, as young
turn away but sit still alongside death covering
their face in disbelief and grief of the life just lost

What is left to wonder if not when it will end?
But which sound is louder?
The *corridos* or the gunshots?

Linda Romero

Pink Shorts

The neighbor girl in bright pink shorts looks out her living
room window and sees retired red, white and blue ... his car

returned across the street. Bags with oranges or grapefruits on neighboring
doorsteps signal his presence nearby. Yellowed prickly grass in front yards

reflect the drought that plagues the Rio Grande Valley. Still, regular visits bring
babysitter's pay and cantaloupe with ice cream to take the sting off the heat.

Today's visit takes mail collected during his week
away. He wears jeans and a blue western shirt.

He's alone.

Rebecca should be back soon.

The girl sits on the couch; sandalwood potpourri breezes throughout the room.
A sick feeling warns her, leave. Her mother waits, she stays.

In a white undershirt and unbelted jeans, the veteran returns
from down the hall, sits on the couch next to her, inches

near. The girl moves farther and farther away until the arm of the sofa presses
against her thigh. He puts his right arm around her neck and his left

hand on her knee and strokes her leg. His hot breath on her face,
You sure have grown up pretty. She squirms free, his grip unlocked. Her heart

pounds and cold fear rushes through her. She trips over the oval
table that allows just enough room for her escape. She runs home.

Days, weeks, months and years pass by and what happened remains unspoken.

She babysits and he continues red, white and blue. The girl never
again wore those pink shorts.

Linda Romero

Sparse

He comes sparse, from a *colonia*
Nearly a town away from county pipelines
Flowing clean water and lakes that don't
Fill of sewer smells and remnants of who
Occupied the land before him.

He quickly eats meals given to him five days
a week, disengaged from conversation from others
Around him, music plugged in their ears, talking
About who they will meet over the weekend.

The monitor dismisses everyone and he goes to class.
The bus ride back is long, but the block and a half walk
Home goes by fast. He stops at a mere structure,
Unsheltered by everything except the wood frame
Behind the tattered sheet covered space.

The taste of metal lingers on his tongue from partially
Eaten pizza slices and cleaned-out tin cups dug
From dumpsters; river water for drinking and bathing
Pools torn clothes around his blistered feet from walking
Hard, broken soil beneath them. The drought

Engulfs his entire existence. A lone child lives on a land
Where no government rules but none to speak for him either.
He looks past where he stands, ankle-deep in his surroundings.

Linda Romero

The Fall of Bagdad[1]

Don Pedro wakes this autumn day,
Descends the stairs to his bar,
And wiping down the rough-hewn wood,
Prepares to pour the drinks.

For years his cantina thrived on gold
That cotton transport culled
From slaves that Texas cruelly worked
Throughout the Civil War.

In fact, all Bagdad grew fat on their blood
Despite Old Mexico's Laws.
Confederate cash, international trade:
The marketplace crushed all ideals.

Once camels and carts lined the streets
Of this town at the river's mouth.
The Gulf fairly teemed with Southern ships
That waited months for their loads.

But two long years have come and gone,
And Bagdad begins to decline:
Just pirates and desperadoes now
Who wallow in waning filth.

---

[1] In 1867, the Mexican town of Bagdad was completely leveled by a hurricane that seemed to spring up overnight. That port at the mouth of the Río Grande had served as the major shipping point for Confederate cotton during the Civil War, cotton cultivated by slaves in Texas and throughout the South. This ballad speculates about the storm that avenged that crime.

Don Pedro throws open the shutters.
A wind swirls in from the south.
A line of black obscures the horizon
Above the bruise-colored sea.

A sudden gust brings the stench
Of rotten fish and disease,
And silhouetted at the door
Appears the Harbinger.

"We're closed right now," the owner says,
"But if you have the coin
And do not mind a little wait,
I'll serve you when I'm done."

The figure steps into the light.
His unkempt hair is long.
He's dressed in Middle-Eastern robes.
His skin and eyes are brown.

His gaze surveys the grimy bar,
Dispassionate and grim.
"I am not come to sample vice:
I come to wipe it out."

Don Pedro has to smile at this.
"So many men have tried,
But here the law obeys but gold:
The mayor's and criminals' greed."

The stranger walks up to the man—
He stinks of fetid flesh—
And with his ancient, spectral voice
Intones his harsh decree:

"Each soul in Bagdad dies today
Whose love for greed is such
That they have wrought another's death
Or profited from slaves.

"Behold the Harbinger of Doom
Is come to bring your end,
To raze your city to the ground,
To drown all evil fiends."

Before Don Pedro can object,
The stranger takes his arm
And with ineluctable grip
He leads him outside.

There by the docks the boats now rock;
The white waves beat their hulls.
To south and east the sky is black
The evening sun bleeds red.

"For eighteen hundred years have I
Perambulated wide,
A tool of vengeance for the one
Who brought me back to life.

"Know'st *Lazarus*? That is my name:
Immortal living dead.
I sank Port Royal to the depths
I heralded the Plague."

He thrusts a skeletal hand toward the sky
And snarls in some guttural tongue.
The air, encumbered with unseen force,
Begins to writhe and thrum.

Like hounds that race at their master's call
To chase and trap their prey,
Across the waves the gray squalls howl
To burst against the town.

Don Pedro gapes in wordless dread
As sails grow fat with wind;
Like men in nooses, shop signs swing,
And loose tiles pelt the ground.

The gale's moan rises to a scream
That's underscored by cracks
As masts are sundered from their keels
And ships flung on the docks.

Pedro struggles to break free,
He longs to bar the door,
To close the shutters one by one
Against the tempest's wrath,

But Lazarus won't let him go,
He draws him closer still.
The storm surge flows about their feet,
Sucking at their clothes.

A cloud of seagulls rushes past
In harsh, infernal din:
Bleached psychopomps that come to drag
A thousand souls to hell.

"Release me, please!" Don Pedro begs
As rain begins to fall
In thick, opaque and frigid shrouds
That obliterate the world.

"I'm innocent!" the taverner screams
To the ancient, ruthless being,
And eldritch eyes bore to his soul
Regarding every crime.

"Where are thy daughters, Pedro Sainz?
What didst thou with those girls?
On their backs in some house of ill repute
To pay the debts thou ow'st.

"Thy drunkenness and lechery
Drove thy wife to suicide.
Art rotten to thy very core,
And like the rest, shalt pay."

Then with a shriek the roof is torn
In ragged chunks from the bar;
Adobe's blasted from the walls;
The storm claws at the bricks.

All around the shanties quake,
They collapse into splintered ruin.
Naught withstands but Lazarus,
Implacable as fate.

The waters wrap them roundabout
As graveclothes seal the dead,
The ancient man dives to the depths,
With Pedro in his arms.

Amidst the wreckage of his town,
Which eddies roil and swirl,
He sees the bodies of his girls,
Like flotsam, twist and turn.

He opens wide his mouth to scream
And water fills his lungs.
The Harbinger releases him.
The bleak world fades away.

But then he's snatched from out his corpse
By Lazarus' deft hand
And lifted high above the earth
To view the scene below:

The waters are receding now,
There's nothing left but sand
And wine-black water stretching forth
To the horizon's edge.

The gulls have gathered thickly,
In each beak a damaged soul,
And they soar into the darkness
Dragging every fiend beyond.

David Bowles

Contributor Biographies

Alan Oak

has been writing poems since the fourth grade, when he wrote a poem about George Washington that deftly rhymed "crossing the Delaware" with "losing his underwear." He's been writing and smart-alecking along ever since. A regular reader at Valley poetry events, Oak has recently had poems, essays and articles published in *Boundless, Women Writers, Journal of South Texas English Studies, Writers of the Rio Grande* and *Extrapolation.* He is an English instructor at the University of Texas at Brownsville, editor for Otras Voces Publishing, and master of ceremonies for the Brownsville Pasta, Poetry and Vino. He has also been self-publishing near-daily poems on twitterbard.com, which now has more than 400 posted "twitterpoems."

David Bowles

An educator and writer from the RGV, Bowles is the author of several books, including the short story collection *The Seed: Stories from the River's Edge* (2011) and the illustrated bilingual encyclopedia of legendary creatures *Mexican Bestiary* (2012). Additionally, he has served as editor for the *Along the River* anthology series, the newly illustrated *Stories That Must Not Die* reprint series, *Donna Hooks Fletcher: Life and Writings* and the magazine *Flashquake.* His book review column Top Shelf appears each Thursday in *The Monitor*, a regional newspaper.

Michael Pacheco

A former attorney-turned-author, Pacheco's debut novel, *The Guadalupe Saints*, was published by Paraguas Books in April 2011; his novella *Seeking Tierra Santa* was released in May 2011. He has had short stories published in *The Gold Man Review, Label Me Latina, The Acentos Review, Boxfire Press, Red Ochre Press* and *AirplaneReading*.

Alejandro Fernández Cabada

writes poetry and short stories. His work has been published in a diverse series of publications in Mexico and the US. Proud of his Mexican heritage, promotes the Spanish language in the Valley through his literary work and music. He has a BA in Spanish and is currently pursuing a Masters in Spanish Literature at the University of Texas Pan American. He is the author of *Escarlata: Un libro de poemas* (2009) and *Días de púrpura* (2012), the first two books in the Colors Trilogy, both from Editora Campamocha.

Daniel Tyx

Daniel Tyx teaches English at South Texas College in McAllen, where he lives with his wife and children. He has had work published in *Along the River 2011, Gettysburt Review* and *Gulf Coast*.

Brianda Salinas

At twenty years of age, Brianda knows where she stands in life. Her very existence is driven by passion and runs on success. She was raised on both sides of the border, and has seen it all. A student at the University of Texas Pan-American, she aspires to be an English teacher and harbors a dream of writing for *Vogue*. She is a woman of many shades—always learning, always morphing.

Rob Johnson

Dr. Johnson is a Professor of English at the University of Texas Pan American. He is the author of *The Lost Years of William S. Burroughs: Beats in South Texas* (Texas A & M University, 2006) and the editor of *Fantasmas: Supernatural Stories by Mexican-American Writers* (Bilingual Press, 2001). He teaches courses on south Texas literature and frequently writes and lectures on border issues.

Robert Paul Moreira

Robert Paul Moreira received his MFA from the University of Texas-Pan American in 2010. Currently, he is an English Ph.D. candidate at the University of Texas-San Antonio researching alterity and constructed identities in sports fiction, films, and performance. His fiction, interviews, criticism, and scholarship have been published or are forthcoming in a variety of venues, including *Bluestem, Aethlon: Journal of Sports Literature, Storyglossia, Breakwater Review, Emprise Review, Metazen,* and the anthologies *SOL: Vol. I* (SOL, 2012) and *New Border Writing* (Texas A&M Press, 2013). He is editor of the forthcoming print anthology *Arriba Baseball!: A Collection of Latino/a Baseball Fiction* (VAO Publishing, 2013) and the recipient of two graduate fiction awards from the Texas Association of Creative Writing Teachers in 2009 and 2010, as well as the Wendy Barker Creative Writing Award in 2011. He serves as head intern for *American Letters and Commentary* and teaches writing and literature at the University of Texas-Pan American.

Erika Said Izaguirre

Erika Said Izaguirre is a Mexican writer born and raised in Tampico, Tamaulipas. She attended the University of Chihuahua, where she earned a degree in Spanish Literature. Her poetry and short stories have been published in Mexican newspapers, magazines and books, including the anthologies "Overview of Young Mexican Poetry," "Women's Cry: Rebel Poetry," "Poetry of Chaos," "The Voice That Sprouts: a Tamaulipas Poetry Retrospective" and "Hell is a Caress." She won first place in the bi-national short story contests of the UTB "Letras en el Estuario" and an honorable mention in Tamaulipa's state short story contest "Rosa de Castaño." She has lived in El Paso, McAllen and San Antonio where she's presently enrolled in the Master of Arts in Spanish program at the UTSA.

Angelo Bowles

is the author of the locally popular children's series *Swift the Cat-Human*. The third volume, *Creep-Out*, was released in October 2012.

Minne Vásquez

is a mother, teacher, and writer. A home-grown resident of the Valley, she writes about events that have impacted her deeply.

Rolando Villafuerte

Born and raised in Rockford, IL, Rolando came to know poetry as an outlet and a form of expression. Having endured various struggles and hardships, he found peace and contentment in the collaboration of words. Now residing in the Rio Grand Valley, Rolando is married with 3 beautiful kids. He continues to write but has also expanded his poetry into the arena of hip-hop with the intent to spread a message of hope and overcoming life's circumstances and issues. The struggles and hardships which were once Rolandos burdens have now become his biggest blessings. His work has appeared in *Boundless* 2012.

G.G. García

is a retired, private management consultant and freelance writer who has worked in the industry since 1972. García has considerable experience in business and government at local, state, national and international levels. He served as a private consultant, a White House aide, senior staff assistant to Governor Clements and as a city administrator for Mercedes, Texas. Valley-born and raised, he wrote a column for the Mercedes Enterprise recalling his days in the Valley. A collection of these columns was printed as *Recuerdos de Ayer*. He continues to work as a freelance writer while living in Amboy, Illinois.

Kathy Trenfield Raines

Kathy grew up in Lubbock, Texas, then Muncie, Indiana. She has lived, raised sons and taught English in the Rio Grande Valley for 31 years. She has enjoyed discussing literature and helping students with writing for over thirty years. She has written since childhood but got a jumpstart through the New Jersey and National Writing Projects. She loves acting, reading, playing music, enjoying nature and visiting friends, family, and pets.

Vanessa Brown

was born in 1982 in Mission, Texas. Educated at Texas A & M University – Kingsville, she returned to La Joya to teach. She married Coke Brown and has three lovely daughters. Her vocation is education and she has a Masters in Educational Administration from Grand Canyon University. Her passion is promoting Arts in the Rio Grande Valley and building a legacy of culture and creativity for her children. She is the author of *Twiffler: A Collection of Poetry* (2012).

Diana Elizondo

Diana is a graduate student in the English program. Born and raised in southern Texas, her goal in life is to become a published writer and poet. She has appeared at many poetry readings throughout the RGV.

Yaresy Salinas

Yary Salinas is a Hispanic female poet from Mission, Texas. She has participated in various poetry events such as "Letras en el estuario" and "Los santos días de la poesía." Her fresh, mischievous poetry is mainly influenced by passion, music, and science. It is saturated with surreal images, unexpected juxtapositions, and brazen metaphors.

Edward Vidaurre

born in East L.A., has been featured in the June 7, 2011, *La Bloga* "On-Line Floricanto" issue; the Valley International Poetry Festival anthology, *Boundless* 2011; and *Writers of the Rio Grande*. He will be published in *The Beatest State in the Nation*, an anthology of Texas Beat poetry forthcoming by UT Press in 2012. Vidaurre is the founder of Pasta, Poetry and Vino.

Nina Medrano

Nina Marie (Bone) Medrano was born and raised in Barryton, Michigan. In 2002, she came on vacation to Mission Texas to visit some friends of her family. She enjoyed her stay there so much that she did not return to Michigan until 2005 and that was only to retrieve her belongings. Since then she has made the Río Grande Valley her home and adds her voice to the chorus when people say, "I wasn't born here, but I got here as quick as I could."

Juventino Manzano

grew up and graduated high school in the Rio Grande Valley. He has been writing for most of his life and has been published in various places including the literary journals of every university he attended (UT Pan American, the former Southwest Texas, and Illinois State University). At Illinois State he had the pleasure of studying creative writing under Ricardo Cortez Cruz and David Foster Wallace. He was nominated for a Push Cart award in 2008 for his poem *I have a Godfather*. Other publishing credits include the *Post Amerikan, Celebrate the Self, Armageddon Buffet, Poets wear Prada, Propergander, Le Petite Bourgeoise, Last Stop at Union Station* among others. He has independently published various works and is currently working on a novel concerning *narco* culture in the Rio Grande Valley and Northeastern Mexico as well as collaborating with an artist on converting one of his stories to a graphic novel format.

Héctor Gómez

A writer based in South Texas, Héctor recently published the second issue of "The Legacy Valley of Tears," an ongoing graphic novel series based in the fictional border town of Cuatro Esquinas, Texas. His "Tejanese" style of beat poetry has been accepted to two anthologies set for 2012 publication, *The Beatest State in the Union: An Anthology of Texas Beat Poets* (UT Press) and *Interstice* (South Texas College Publications). He lives in San Juan, Texas, with his wife and two children.

Valeria Espinoza

Currently teaching at Donna High School, Valeria Espinoza was born and raised in South Texas, the Rio Grande Valley. Initially studying to become a Music Director at Texas A&M University – Kingsville (TAMUK), she quickly realized her passion was in writing. She then transferred to the University of Texas – Pan American (UTPA), in Edinburg, Texas, where she received her Bachelors in English in 2011. She enjoys teaching her students, whom she calls her "kiddos," because she states they "allow [her] to be [herself]: completely silly." Her childhood, students, spontaneous late night runs to Wal-Mart, and current life are what inspires her to write. Ms. Emmy Perez and Dr. Amy Cummins, professors at UTPA, introduced her to the world of creative writing and young adult literature. "It's because of them two that I write today." Ms. Espinoza resides in McAllen, TX with her grandmother and her hyper terrier named Lulu. She loves traveling, playing video games, watching *Ghost Adventures*, animals (in every shape and size), and evidently, writing: flash fiction, short stories, and poems.

Christopher Carmona

A beat poet following in the tradition of beat poets like Jack Kerouac, Bob Kaufman, and Raul Salinas, Christopher believes in practicing poetry as a form of social resistance. He was a nominee for the Alfredo Cisneros de Miral Foundation Award for Emerging Writers in 2011 and has been published in *The Writers' Block, Beatlick Art & News, World Audience Literary Journal, Tecolote, Boundless: The Rio Grande Valley International Poetry Festival Anthology 2011* and *2012, La Bloga, The Houston Poetry Festival 2011 Anthology, Vandal, phati'tude Literary Magazine, Sagebrush Review*, and *MEZCLA*. His first book of poetry entitled *beat* is published by Slough Press. He is also editing an anthology of Beat Texas writings called *The Beatest State in the Union* with Chuck Taylor and Rob Johnson. Currently he is working on his second book of poetry titled *I Have Always Been Here*, which explores being a Chican@ beat poet. He is the organizer of the Annual Beat Poetry and Arts Festival.

Leopoldo Farías

Leo says, "Poetry is my coping mechanism it is something I most use to help make sense of this world and my experience. Poetry is the most passionate and authentic way of sharing with others. For me it's my way of sharing the more complex parts of myself and for me the gratitude comes in the chance of putting the words out there for others to read."

Edwin de Kock

Edwin de Kock (1930-), a polyglot immigrant, is a famous Esperanto poet with ten volumes of original poetry to his credit. His *Sub fremdaj ĉieloj* (*Under Foreign Skies*), 2007, contains several poems with Hispanic and related themes. He has also published in English and Afrikaans. One of his other passions is the study of history and prophecy. In this genre, his latest work, *The Truth about 666,* comprises more than 850 pages. It appeared as a digital publication in 2011. De Kock was a professional educator for more than thirty-five years in South Africa, Korea, and the United States. He finished this career by teaching writing at the University of Texas, Pan American, Edinburg, from 1996 to 2000.

Katherine Hoerth

is the author of *The Garden Uprooted* (Slough Press, 2012), a collection of poetry, and two chapbooks titled *Among the Mariposas* (Mouthfeel Press, 2010) and *The Garden of Dresses* (Mouthfeel Press, 2012). She teaches writing at the University of Texas Pan American and serves as Assistant Poetry Editor of *Fifth Wednesday Journal*. Her work has been published in numerous journals including *Borderlands: Texas Poetry Review, Front Porch*, and *Boxcar*.

Sylvia Pérez

A writer of adult science fiction, Sylvia has published *To Save the Humans, The Record Keeper's Wife*, and *Salphos: Prince of Delnot*.

Erika Garza

aka La Erika or Poeta Power, is a local loca/colocha/word-witch. Her lists of accomplishments include, but are not limited to wife, mother, editor, lecturer, and some other stuff.

Juan Antonio González

is a poet, narrator, and literary critic. His academic works, spanning several decades, have been published in a diversity of journals in the U.S., Latin America, and Spain. He has published poetry and prose in the following books: *Itineransias*, Ed. LAGO 2008; *Letras en el Estuario*, Ed. ALJA 2008; *Antología Canicular*, Ed. Campamocha 2009; *Voces desde el Casamata*. Ed. ALJA 2010; *Encuentro de poesía Río Grande/ Río Bravo*, Ed. ALJA 2011; *Antología Invernal*, Ed. Campamocha 2011; and *Antología de poesía sobre poesía*, Ed. ALJA 2012. In press at this time are his books of poems *Tesituras del silencio* and *Memorias del olvido*, as well as his collection of short stories, *Taxidermia en vivo*. Presently, he works as a Professor of Hispanic letters, Creative Writing and Translation at the University of Texas at Brownsville and Texas Southmost College, where since 1996 he has served as Editor-in-Chief of the literary journal *Novosantanderino* and the student publication *De Puño y Letra*. He currently holds editorial appointments at the following journals: *Puentes*, Arizona State University; and *Pegaso*, the University of Oklahoma at Norman.

Claudia D. Hernández

Claudia D. Hernández was born and raised in Guatemala. She holds a BA in Liberal Studies with a minor in Art and a BCLAD teaching credential. She is a bilingual educator in the city of Los Angeles and is currently finishing a Masters in Multicultural Education. Beginning in June of 2012, Claudia will attend Antioch University in pursuit of her MFA in Creative Writing for Young Adults and Children's Literature. She writes, illustrates, and manually binds children's books. She has written six children's stories, one of which (*Julia Always Knew—Julia Siempre Supo*) has been integrated into the curriculum for **It's OK to Be Different**, a comprehensive elementary school program in the State of New Jersey that teaches children tolerance and respect for people who are different. Her photography, poetry, and short stories have been published in *The Indigenous Sovereignty Issue of The Peak, Hinchas de Poesía, Chicana in the Midst, Poets Responding to SB1070*, La Bloga's on-line *Floricanto, KUIKATL ~ A XicanIndio Literary and Arts Journal*, and in the first anthology of *Colectivo Verso Activo*.

Rossy Evelin Lima

Rossy Evelin Lima is currently getting her PhD in Linguistics from the University of Houston. She has been published in four antologies in Mexico and de United States *La Ruta de los Juglares* (McAllen) *Letras en el Estuario* (Matamoros) *La mujer rota* (Jalisco) and *El Retorno* (Edinburg).

José Hernandez Díaz

has been published in *The Best American Nonrequired Reading Anthology 2011, Bombay Gin Literary Journal, The Progressive Magazine, Kuikatl Journal, Poetry Flash, La Gente Newsmagazine, 3:AM Magazine* (UK), *Tan lejos de dios* (MEX), *The Delinquent* (UK), *El norte que viene* (ESP), *ditch poetry* (CAN), *Blood Lotus Journal, Huizache Literary Magazine, Counterexample Poetics, BlazeVOX12*, among others. He is an MFA candidate at Antioch University Los Angeles, where he serves as co-poetry editor of *Lunch Ticket*. In addition, he has edited five novels for Floricanto Press.

Rachel Vela

has been writing poetry since her adolescent years. She is the founder of WE NEED WORDS, a poetry/open-mic event that seeks to celebrate local poets, musicians and artists. Rachel has been in love all her life; her loves are England, poetry, books, the 6th train to Union Square and red wine...in Central Park.

Amalia Ortiz

Amalia Ortiz is a Tejana performance poet and playwright who has appeared on three seasons of Russell Simmons Presents Def Poetry on HBO and the NAACP Image Awards on FOX. She has toured colleges and universities as a solo artist and with the performance-poetry troupes Diva Diction, the Chicano Messengers of Spoken Word, and the Def Poetry College Tour. She was awarded a writing residency at the National Hispanic Cultural Center. She is a Canto-Mundo Fellow and a Hedgebrook writer-in-residence alumna, where she wrote a Latino musical, *Carmen de la Calle.*

Kristin Keith

Kristin says of herself, "A 2003 graduate of the University of Kentucky, I moved to the Rio Grande Valley in 2008. It was at this time that I changed careers and entered the education field. God blessed me with a classroom in Donna, Texas, where I am currently in my fourth year of teaching. In my free time I enjoy reading a good book, spending time with my friends and family, and working with the kids at my church."

María Piedra

María says of herself, "I was born in Nuevo Progreso, Tamaulipas, Mexico (otherwise known as *Las Flores*). I came to the USA when I was 17 years old. I love to read, write, sing and talk. I am a creative elementary teacher who is NOT *'Waiting for Superman'* but *becoming Superman* regardless of school politics. I believe in teaching with love. I have God as the author of my life, and I believe in him because nobody has given or offered more than what He has. Writing has giving me the opportunity to collaborate and be the coauthor of life. I am inspired by authors... need a coauthor?"

César de León

Born in Monterrey, Nuevo Leon, César moved to the Rio Grande Valley at the age of 4 and has lived here for 35 years. As a native of South Texas and a writer, he feels a duty to explore and showcase the rich experience of living along the border of two great nations. He will be graduating soon from UTPA with a BA in English, and he plans to pursue an MFA in Creative Writing and a Graduate Certificate in Mexican American Studies. Most recently, his poetry has been published in UTPA's *Gallery* magazine.

Clarrissia Nerio

Clarrissia is a romanticist with a passion for poetry and art. She has been writing confessional poetry since she was 15. For over the past 10 years, she has been working towards more publications and has become very dedicated to her writing. She has two great loves in her life: poetry and her one and only son.

Yolanda López

Yolanda López discovered her passion for writing poetry and short story as a young girl. Her work emerged in her recent participation at the 2011 National Novel Writing Month, South Texas College's *Tierra Firme* and *Interstice* publications and VIPF: *Boundless* 2012.

Linda Romero

Linda is from Harlingen, TX, and has been published in the *Boundless* 2010 and *Boundless* 2012 anthologies. She coordinates Vidas Cruzadas, a creative writing workshop at El Milagro Clinic in McAllen for Life Center. Linda is currently working on her MFA in Creative Writing at UTPA.